C000175696

Praise for *Frazzled to Fab*

'Tamara, what a brilliant book this will be, and how amazingly helpful to frazzled mums everywhere! I wish it had existed when I had my babies! You're an absolute star to have seen the need and produced the text – not an easy thing to do at all, but it will reward you both emotionally and financially when it flies off the shelves.'

Sally Sutton

'I thoroughly recommend Tamara's system. I really did feel so much benefit from doing the EFT every day and Tamara is a guiding light throughout it all. Very uplifting and only take around 5 minutes a session, but I noticed that on the very odd day I didn't do it how much more easily I could become frazzled/anxious. It is now something I want to incorporate into my life and I am managing so far. I have previously done Transcendental Meditation, but find I get the same positive results from tapping but it takes much less time.'

Julie Thomson

'As a business-owner, home schooler, & wife to a husband with limiting disabilities this system spoke to my feeling of CONSTANTLY being overwhelmed. Sometimes that overwhelm led to feelings of hopelessness, that I'll never get ahead, and feelings of resentment that I never get a break. I experienced occasional insomnia, fatigue, depression... I was a bit concerned that even this system would feel overwhelming but I KNEW it would be helpful...AND IT WAS. Tamara led tapping on topics including feeling overwhelmed, shifting perspective, focusing on gratitude and other emotions. I even discovered that I had feelings of guilt that I was unaware of, buried below my consciousness! The tapping helped me recognize it AND resolve those feelings so I could productively address what caused the feelings of guilt. This system was so beneficial in itself, and it also confirmed to me the value of Tapping.'

Jamie Lynn Fisher

'I have been following Tamara's system and I can't rave enough about it. All of that stress and chaos that you feel is insurmountable becomes manageable in a very calming way. It was life-changing for me in so many ways.'

Natalie Bachiri

FRAZZLED

to

Fabulous

in 5 Minutes a Day

Regain your calm

Enjoy your kids

Get more done

Tamara Donn

DONN
Publishing

First published in 2021 by Donn Publishing

Copyright Tamara Donn 2021

ISBN: 978-1-9168853-7-0

All rights reserved. No part of this publication may be reproduced, distributed, or transmitted in any form or by any means, including photocopying, recording, or other electronic or mechanical methods, without the prior written permission of the author, except in the case of brief quotations embodied in critical reviews and certain other non-commercial uses permitted by copyright law.

Illustrations by Keona Donn

Edited by Sally Sutton

Book cover and layout by Jen Parker at Fuzzy Flamingo
www.fuzzyflamingo.co.uk

www.frazzledtofabulous.com

Facebook: @TamaraDonnEFT

Instagram: @TamaraDonnEFT

To Peter, who planted the seed in my mind that I had a book inside me that needed to be written, and never stopped reminding me to get on with it until I actually finished it!

For Keona, who made me a mum and showed me how much joy, love and fun life can bring.

Acknowledgments

Writing this book has been a labour of love, and I could not have done it without the support of Peter, my husband, my soulmate, and my business partner. My gratitude goes to him for jointly writing the Quick Guide to EFT chapter with me.

A big thank you goes to my daughter Keona, who created the illustrations. We spent a sunny week at my parents' house by the sea, enjoying morning walks by the beach as we created a persona for Molly, our adorable stressed mum, and her children, who feature in the daily chapters.

I could not have written this book without the hundreds of mums who took part in my online 'Get My Sanity Back' challenge, on which this book is based. Their feedback about their incredible transformations is the reason I want to shout from the rooftops that mums don't have to live a stressed and overwhelmed life. There IS another way! It's simple, and it simply requires you to put yourself first for just five minutes a day. Thank you to the mums, some of whose names and details have been changed, whose feedback is included in this book. Thank you to the mums whose stories I have shared. And thank you to the mums who thoroughly tested out the tapping scripts and read the book, offering constructive feedback.

A big thank you goes to Sally Sutton, who meticulously edited my book, gave me loads of encouragement and guided me gently to help it flow better, Talya Stone, who kindly wrote the foreword, Jen Parker who created the beautiful look of the book and Eleanor Hatherley and Lucy Blunden for meticulously proofreading.

Writing this book has been a long, drawn out journey, and so many coaches, EFT practitioners, business buddies and friends have motivated, encouraged and supported me along the way, in particular my gratitude goes to Eleanor Hatherley, Jas Dale, Ruth Wood, Michelle Mahal (formerly Holmes), Sarah Sienkiewicz and Alison Jones. Thank you all.

Foreword

You would think that being a mum would be the easiest thing in the world, wouldn't you? After all, we have been doing this motherhood thing since the beginning of time. Well thanks to the modern day pressures exerted on us by society of trying to do it all, be it all, and have it all, this couldn't be further from the truth!

Mums these days are under the greatest amount of pressure than they have ever experienced in the timeline of motherdom. In fact, the article on my website that gets the most hits pretty much every day is "15 things to do when you feel like a bad mum". I think that says it all.

Being a mum is hard – even those who look like they are gliding through life are in fact probably struggling on some level. There are more and more demands on our mental bandwidth and, at the time of writing during the pandemic, a mum's mental load is heavier than ever.

But what happens when that load just keeps getting heavier? In the end, we simply just crash and burn. I know, because I have been there and done that — putting too much pressure on myself in motherhood, as a woman, as a partner, in my career. The list goes on. There is only so long you can keep going before you totally unravel.

We already know that mental health is an incredibly fragile area among new mothers, but the problem doesn't simply go away as your children get older. Often it evolves into something else. And that something else is stress.

Mums everywhere are suffering with everyday stress as they struggle to deal with everything that gets thrown at them. Some studies show that as many as two thirds of mums believe that stress affects their ability to be a good parent — something I know to be true first hand.

We can't go on like this. Mums more than ever need the tools and techniques to cope with the stress of being a mother in these modern times. We need to prioritise self-care and make it mandatory. It is not selfish to look after yourself. In fact I would go so far as to say it is non-negotiable if you want to maintain your mental and physical health and avoid heading into a personal crisis of sorts.

Having spiralled down to the depths of burnout myself – and having to deal with the ramifications this had on my mental and physical health — I learnt this all the hard way. If only I had had the wake up call before it was too late. There would undoubtedly be things that would be different in my life now. Things I would no longer feel guilty about. And as for that modern day blight of mum guilt — well that deserves a whole foreword of its own!

But thankfully now, you are here with this book in your hands, wanting to change something in your life before you spiral down further. You are incredible! You know that something is not right, and that it needs to be fixed. And thankfully, you have the right guide to help you navigate this new important phase in your motherhood journey – this book! So give yourself a pat on the back for getting this far.

I have experienced first hand the incredible effects of EFT and tapping. It is a phenomenal tool for dealing with everyday stress and overwhelm, and your best friend in processing and managing your emotions whether they are minor irritations throughout the day or big sweeping tsunamis of overwhelm. Even better, it really is true that its transformative effects can be harnessed in just five minutes a day. After 30 days of using this book, if my personal experience of EFT and tapping is anything to go by, I'm confident you will feel lighter, brighter, more in control, less chaotic and most importantly less frazzled.

Talya Stone, creator of the leading digital parenting magazine
motherhoodtherealdeal.com

Introducing Molly

Meet Molly! She's a stressed, overwhelmed and exhausted mum. She loves her children more than anything, but they never get the best of her. Her partner, Gary, doesn't feature much in this book because he's always at work, leaving Molly to hold the home fort. She often feels resentful and like a single mum. Being a mum life often feels like a continuous hamster wheel that's impossible to get off.

Keona and I created Molly and her children, Lulu and Harry, on our morning walks. We have become very fond of her, and this page is dedicated to her and all the mums struggling with the frazzledness of motherhood.

Contents

PART 1: Preparation   1

    A request from the author   3

    Introduction   4

    Hitting the ground running:

        Is there another option?   4

    How is this approach different?   12

    A Quick Guide to EFT: What is EFT?   14

    The Quick-start Tapping Guide   23

PART 2: The Challenge   29

    Introduction   31

    Charlotte's story: How EFT

        helped newly single mum   36

PART 3: Your Next 30 Days   39

    Day 1   41

    Day 2   46

    Day 3   50

    Day 4   56

    Day 5   64

    Day 6   69

    Harriet's story: EFT has transformed

        this mum's experience of parenting   75

    Day 7   77

    Day 8   81

    Day 9   87

    Day 10   92

    Day 11   98

    Day 12   104

    Day 13   111

    S-J's story: EFT helped

        my children get to sleep   117

Day 14 119
Day 15 122
Day 16 129
Day 17 135
Day 18 142
Day 19 149
Day 20 155
Elizabeth Mary's story:
    Birth trauma gone in 20 minutes 161
Day 21 163
Day 22 166
Day 23 173
Day 24 180
Day 25 188
Day 26 194
Day 27 200
Silva and Bronte's story:
    Three generations of EFT 206
Day 28 208
Day 29 211
Day 30 216

PART 3: Moving Forward 225
Introduction 227
Your children and EFT: Introduction 232
Teresa's story
    Surrogate Tapping 251
Next steps 253
Troubleshooting 259
Further resources 275
About Tamara 277

Appendix: Tapping scripts 281

Disclaimer

All the materials and linked online resources in this book are provided for informational and educational purposes only and are not intended to be or to serve as a substitute for professional medical advice, examination, diagnosis or treatment. Always seek the advice of your doctor or other qualified health provider with regard to any questions you may have about a medical or psychological condition. Never disregard professional medical advice or delay in seeking it because of information you access in or through any portion of this book.

EFT (Emotional Freedom Techniques) or Tapping is very powerful and can lead to significant emotional shifts. This could mean suppressed emotions surfacing. If you have been diagnosed with mental illness or any other illness or disorder that puts you or others at risk, you are strongly advised not to attempt tapping alone for self-help initially and to seek advice from your doctor or a qualified EFT practitioner. Similarly, if you feel concerned that you may not be able to support yourself or deal with particular issues or feelings that may surface, you are advised to see a qualified EFT practitioner, or at least to get in touch with one in case you need support at short notice. You proceed at your own risk, and the author cannot be held responsible for any undesirable outcome resulting from using the processes described in this book.

Tapping using the material and links in this book is at your sole risk. The information provided is 'as is' and is offered without any representation or warranties of any kind.

The testimonials and opinions expressed by the mums who have shared their experiences and stories are genuine. In some cases names or details have been changed to protect their privacy. The testimonials and opinions expressed by the mums who have shared their experiences and stories are genuine, and I include them to illustrate the many ways in which EFT has worked for my clients. In some cases I have changed names or details to protect their privacy.

PART 1
Preparation

A request from the author

Frazzled to Fabulous in Five Minutes a Day is a unique and original process that is the loving culmination of many years of working with mums and witnessing their incredible transformations. Please immerse yourself in the experience and create the life you want for yourself and your family. If you love it, feel free to share the book with friends and clients as you would want your own work to be shared.

Please read and enjoy *Frazzled to Fabulous in Five Minutes a Day* as a book or ebook. However, please don't reproduce any part of this book: please credit me, tag me, and share a link to my website, Frazzledtofabulous.com, whenever you mention or reference my work.

With deep gratitude

Tamara x

Introduction

Hitting the ground running: Is there another option?

Is this your typical morning?

* You've overslept because you spent the night worrying about your to-do list
* You rush your children to get ready for school
* You lose your temper with your child for refusing to put on a coat
* On the way to school you just avoid an accident because you're distracted by your children arguing in the back of the car
* You arrive at school stressed and irritated

❀ You arrive at work late, still carrying the stress of the morning school run

My 30-Day Challenge will help you to create the following as a possible alternative scenario:

❀ If you wake up in the night thinking about your to-do list, you spend five minutes tapping, which sends you back to sleep
❀ On hearing your alarm, you spend five minutes tapping to help you feel refreshed, present and available to your children
❀ If you're triggered by your child, eg because he or she refuses to put on their coat, you spend five minutes in the loo tapping so that you can deal with the situation calmly
❀ If your children start arguing in the car, you remind them of their tapping fingers and guide them through a mini tapping routine

This kind of morning leaves you feeling relaxed and prepared for your day ahead!

You may be thinking 'Yeah, right! Does she live in cloud cuckoo land?! She doesn't know what it's really like.'

For over ten years I've been helping hundreds of mums in situations both similar to and different from yours to regain their calm, enjoy their children more, and get more done.

And not only that: they have experienced some surprising and unexpected side effects affecting all areas of life, which I go into detail about later.

Most of my clients are stressed mothers who feel that they never have enough time. But they don't often seek me out for this reason: most accept that that's how life is. They meet other mothers at the school gates who are experiencing similar challenges and they don't know there could be another way. It's often only when they get to breaking point that they realise they can't go on like that and seek help. My desire for you, having found this book, is that you use it to take action now.

Doing the daily challenges will help you:

❀ build resilience in your busy life
❀ reduce the intensity and the number of times you get to breaking point
❀ and increase the number of times you feel fabulous!

In this book I will show you how you can create a great start to your day every day and the cumulative effect of this on all aspects of your life, from improved emotional well-being to more patience with your children and feeling more in control of your life.

So how do I get from frazzled to fabulous?

The 30-Day Challenge will help you take baby steps towards instilling permanent new habits that can create a life of calm and peace so that you can experience and enjoy your life, your family and your work.

Thirty days is a good amount of time to create a new habit, because when we find ourselves in a stressful situation we're unlikely to feel like trying something new and we fall back on our old ways. For example, if we haven't been able to set healthy boundaries between our work and home life, which can be a particular challenge when running a business from home, using willpower alone without changing ingrained habits is hard.

I will help you release the underlying causes of your stress habits – overwhelm, guilt, inappropriate anger, exhaustion, etc – and start to work on creating new, positive structures.

Why do we get stressed and feel unable to cope?

The underlying causes of stress habits may come from childhood experiences.

> One of my one-to-one clients contacted me because she was suffering from insomnia and exhaustion and was feeling overwhelmed. On closer investigation we identified that she was feeling anxious because her son was about to start secondary school. She'd been bullied when she started secondary school herself and wanted to protect him from such an experience.

> We released the trauma of being bullied and her beliefs about herself as a result of that experience. We then did some tapping to resource her with the qualities she needed to feel strong as a mother and able to support her son in his transition. The result was that she felt calmer, more peaceful, and more accepting of his journey, recognising that it would be different from hers. She slept better, felt better during the day, and was more productive at work and more present for her son.

Another mother was experiencing a lot of anger towards her small children. Her own mother had died when she was young, and she'd had to grow up very quickly and learn to be the capable one, always taking care of everyone else. Now she was finding having two young children to take care of and running a business from home too much. She had suppressed her own needs, and her frustration came out as bursts of inappropriate anger towards the children. Once we had released the trauma around her mother dying, she was able to see that it was okay to have needs of her own and to make some changes in her life to start accommodating them. From here, we worked on making tapping a daily habit so that in times of stress in the future she would have it at her fingertips. This resulted in more energy for her business and more enjoyment of her children.

Here are some other interesting effects of tapping that mums have reported:

❀ EFT has become their go-to place at times of stress
❀ They use it as an additional parenting tool
❀ They teach it to their children

Teaching EFT to our children is the area that excites me most, as we're creating a new generation that has this powerful tool at their fingertips! Imagine knowing about this while you were growing up and using it to help yourself with issues such as romantic breakups, exam stress, finding a job, the death of a loved one, divorce, illness etc…

Here's an example of how I was able to use EFT in a personal emergency:

I'd planned a lovely day out in London with my mum treating me to a yummy breakfast at Dolly's in Selfridges. From there we were due to catch a bus to the Imperial War Museum.

Seeing the bus approaching, we started to run for it. My mum tripped over a stone bench and banged her temple. She felt okay, though shaken, but there was a lot of blood, and I'm pleased to say the people around us were very kind and supportive.

As I was wondering what we should do, a Selfridges security guard asked us if we'd like to go to their first aid room, which we did. A very sweet first-aider gave us plasters and tissues for the blood, recommended that we went to A&E and booked and paid for a taxi to take us to University College Hospital.

Although there was a long wait, as expected, all the staff were very helpful and accommodating, and we felt in capable hands. As we were very close to Ainsworths Homoeopathic Pharmacy I headed there to get some remedies for injury and shock. Until that point I'd been in survival mode, only thinking of what needed to be done next. The walk to the pharmacy gave me time to reflect, and a wave of emotions came over me with flashbacks of my mother's fall.

Immediately I used EFT to acknowledge and release the emotions and images in my mind, leaving me feeling calmer and lighter.

When I got back to the hospital the doctor was about to start stitching up the wound. I asked if it would be okay to tap on the tapping points on her fingers as he worked, and he said that he was very open-minded and that anything that helps his patients relax is good for him too. The tapping helped my mother feel calm and relaxed during the procedure, especially when the doctor said that it was bleeding more than expected and called in a consultant to discuss the best approach.

The only time I forgot to tap was when I felt a bit faint at all the blood!

All was well in the end, and my mother made a fast recovery.

I'm sharing this story to demonstrate how EFT has become my habit and go-to place in times of stress. If I hadn't practiced regularly to make it a habit, I wouldn't have had the presence of mind to use it for the stress and shock of the occasion.

In this book I address the commonest reasons why so many mums struggle with stress, overwhelm, anxiety, guilt and exhaustion and find themselves unable to make sustainable, permanent, positive changes.

If you're ready to let go of the blocks that are stopping you from:

❋ looking forward to your day
❋ jumping out of bed in the morning with a spring in your step
❋ getting a good night's sleep
❋ having time for and enjoying your children
❋ being productive with the time you have
❋ and finding calm and ease in your daily life,

and you're ready to commit to carving out just five minutes a day (of the 1440 available!) to create this change, read on to find out how you can lay the foundations for a great relationship with your children, productive use of your time, abundant energy and more than enough time out for yourself – without feeling guilty, undeserving or overwhelmed.

Don't be the mum who continues to drag herself through life because she's resigned herself to that being 'just the way things are', or who tries to change but keeps getting caught up in her busyness.

❋ Be the mum who enjoys her life and being with her children
❋ Be the mum who knows that taking time out for herself means that she has more to give to her children

❀ Be the mum who everyone asks 'How did you change and become so calm, happy and productive?'

❀ Be the mum who takes just five minutes a day for herself

By reading this book you are already taking the first steps to making this your reality!

The method you're about to learn has been proven to create positive, long-lasting results. All you have to do to create the life you want for yourself and your children is to keep reading and put the simple, quick and easy exercises outlined in this book into practice. Take control of your life right now, get your sanity back, and enjoy the new life you're creating!

How is this approach different?

This approach isn't about using willpower or trying to find solutions to your stress, overwhelm and exhaustion. Maybe you've already tried tapping, and although it worked for a while you then reverted to your old ways. Maybe you've given up even before trying, because you feel too trapped or overwhelmed and have resigned yourself to this being the way things are.

Common concerns

No time!

The great news about EFT is that it's so quick to do that even one minute can sometimes be enough to create a little shift, and if that's all the time you have, then better one minute than none!

Too tired!

I understand that when you're tired it can feel almost impossible to motivate yourself to do anything extra. The great news is that you've bought this book, so you've taken the first step. Now all you need to do is to try this technique for at least one minute. If you can do more that's even better. Remember — change can't happen unless you take one small step, and the first step often feels the hardest. You're not alone! I'll support you every step of the way, and if you need more than that you can do this challenge with friends so that you can motivate each other. I also encourage you to join my Facebook support group you can access from Frazzledtofabulous.com/Bonus to use as a source of encouragement and inspiration and meet other mums on the same journey.

It's normal!

Many clients tell me they think stress and exhaustion are a normal part of being a busy mum juggling the school run, work, playdates, pets, partners, their own needs and life in general. Mums tell me they believe they just have to live with it and get on with life. I disagree. People who use EFT as a regular habit experience more ease, calm, lightness and fun in their lives.

A Quick Guide to EFT

What is EFT?

EFT stands for Emotional Freedom Techniques, also known as Tapping. It originates from the Traditional Chinese Medicine system, and has been described as acupuncture without the needles.

It's easy to learn and use, and often produces rapid results. It's suitable and safe to use with babies and children.

It is a simple yet powerful tool to help you release negative beliefs and emotions that you can apply on your own as an empowering DIY technique, or with a practitioner to release deeper-rooted or stubborn issues.

One very significant aspect of EFT that sets it apart from many other treatments, especially emotion-oriented ones, is that it is often possible to experience a shift within minutes. It's not uncommon for practitioners to witness major traumas being released and permanently cleared in one to three sessions. This can push our belief boundaries significantly – read more about this on Day 12 of the challenge on page 104 and in the chapter on Troubleshooting on page 259.

EFT works surprisingly well for most people most of the time, and when used thoroughly its effects are usually found to be permanent. According to Dr Peta Stapleton, the author of *The Science Behind Tapping*, there have been over two million downloads of Gary Craig's *EFT Manual* in English, which is also available in twenty other languages. So it's definitely popular! I've trained staff to use EFT in schools and hospitals, as well as hundreds of individuals who use it both for themselves and in their professions.

When I work with mums I find common themes that they find most challenging come up again and again. The EFT scripts in this book are based primarily on these themes. When using EFT you'll tend to get better results when the wording is based on your specific feelings and what you're working with. As the scripts I offer in this book are not specific to your particular situation, please change the words to match how you feel more accurately. The more personal the words you use are, the more effective the tapping will be. Because of this, tapping using your own words, or with a practitioner who will help you to find them, will give you the best and fastest results. Having said this, hundreds of mums have turned their lives around simply by using my tapping scripts and videos.

To find out more about the professional treatment modalities see the organisations listed under Further resources section on page 275.

Why should I practice EFT for five minutes every day?

Doing one or two rounds of EFT takes as little as five minutes a day, and the incredible thing is that even in such a short time mums report feeling less stressed, less anxious, and calmer, lighter and more energised.

When you commit to tapping for five minutes a day you will find that you:

※ achieve clarity and increase focus
※ release anxiety and nip anger in the bud
※ become more present and available to your children

✳ sleep better
✳ feel more energised and 'morning-ready', even if you slept badly
✳ can calm and relax yourself so that you can be calm for your children
✳ start to use tapping as a parenting tool
✳ and can teach it to your children, giving them a powerful self-help tool to use on anything from aches and pains to upsets, peer pressure, bullying, academic pressure, etc.

Doing EFT every day can have unexpected side effects

These are some of the experiences that my clients have shared after getting into the habit of tapping every day:

✳ I've stopped needing a glass of wine at the end of the day
✳ I've stopped spending money to make myself feel better because I feel so good
✳ My phobia's disappeared
✳ I'm happy again
✳ I've stopped dreading getting up in the morning
✳ I've stopped craving sugar
✳ My period pains disappeared when I tapped every day
✳ I have a reason to get up in the morning again
✳ I'm feeling more loving and connected to my partner
✳ The nausea I've been experiencing for the last eight months has disappeared
✳ I feel happy again my husband asked me what I've been doing to create that change!

'I'm creating a daily habit to release stress and other negative emotions and start creating more calm and ease in my and my son's life. It feels empowering, miraculous, uplifting and comforting to be able to shift my state in just five minutes.'
Laurie

'I did EFT last night ....well I must say, I slept through from midnight to 7.30am!! That's a first in ages!! Also, I haven't napped today, and I've had a full-on day. Thank you so much, Tamara.' Karen

'I can't rave enough about this programme. All of that stress and chaos that you feel is insurmountable becomes manageable in a very calming way. It was life-changing for me in so many ways.' Natalie

How does EFT work?

The amygdala is a part of the brain that's responsible for our survival. It prepares us to deal with emergencies in order to keep us safe. When it detects fear, the amygdala releases stress hormones that cause us to fight, freeze, or flee. This mechanism kept cavemen and women safe from wild animals and other dangers. Nowadays we're physically much safer in our daily lives and don't need to be on high alert all the time, but the truth is that most of us are. There are two types of threat: actual threat, such as dodging a car that doesn't stop when you cross the road, and perceived threat, for instance worrying that your child won't eat enough, isn't safe walking down the road by themselves, or is being bullied.

Many mums have these worries spinning around in their heads day in and day out, sending stress signals to the brain that continually release the fight, flight, or freeze hormone, overriding the prefrontal cortex, which is responsible for reasoning and creative problem-solving. So it's important to be able to calm ourselves. Negative thoughts such as 'I'm running late to pick my child up from school', 'I feel so helpless seeing my child struggle with friendships', or 'What did I do so wrong that's made my children so rude to me?' contribute to stimulating the amygdala to release stress hormones.

How does EFT help? A recent study on its effects on cortisol, the stress hormone, worked with three groups of people: the first had an hour of talk therapy, the second had an hour of EFT, and the third group, the control, had nothing. The researchers were surprised to see that the only group with a statistically significant reduction in cortisol was the EFT group, who experienced an average drop of 24 per cent. Among other things, raised cortisol levels shut down the creative centre in the brain, as it recognises that survival is more important than creativity. It also results in increased irritability, difficulty sleeping, feelings of overwhelm, stress, depleted energy, and holding on to fat! No wonder so many mums feel frazzled so much of the time!

You don't need to know how EFT works for it to work for you; however, understanding some basic information about it can really help motivate you to give it the chance to prove itself to you. After all, if this is the first time you've come across it you're likely to be at least a bit sceptical!

What can I use tapping for?

The list of uses for tapping is endless, but it's best known for dissipating negative emotions such as anger, fear, sadness, anxiety etc. In fact the question here should be 'What *can't* you use tapping for'? Here are some of the things I've successfully used EFT to help mums with:

- ❀ exhaustion and sleep issues
- ❀ stress, overwhelm, anxiety, guilt, and other negative emotions
- ❀ relationship and family challenges
- ❀ limiting beliefs such as 'I'm not good enough', 'I'm alone', 'Life's a struggle'
- ❀ miscarriage trauma
- ❀ abortion trauma
- ❀ menstrual issues

❊ pregnancy fears

❊ preparing to give birth

❊ fertility

❊ birth trauma

❊ post-natal depression

❊ weight loss

❊ new mum issues such as problems with your baby sleeping, feeding, crying, jealous older siblings and even more to cope with

❊ parenting challenges

❊ trauma and upsetting memories

❊ becoming a more productive, more confident and all-round better parent

In this book I will support you as you release the stress in your life so that you can experience more ease, calm, clarity and peace.

One of Gary Craig's (EFT founder) catchphrases is 'Try it on anything': absolutely anything that's causing mental, emotional, spiritual or physical upset or distress is valid material for tapping!

Will EFT work for me?

As an EFT trainer and practitioner since 2009, I have found that many people get great results from tapping along with videos or using scripts. But EFT works fastest and most efficiently when the words you say match exactly how you feel.

Since I don't know you and what you're feeling, I'll be using words that many of my clients relate well to. If you don't relate to them, I recommend altering them to match how you're feeling in the moment more accurately.

So for example if the tapping script says 'I want to release all this stress in my parenting, my work and my relationship,' and you don't have a job or a partner but you do have a stressful relationship with your mum, change it to reflect this, saying for instance 'I want to release all this stress in my parenting and in my relationship with my mum.'

Sometimes, however, using your own words and tapping on your own isn't enough to get great results. If this is the case for you, check the Troubleshooting chapter on page 259 for suggestions on how to improve your results.

I find that around 80 per cent of my one-to-one clients respond to the process very well indeed. For another 10 to 15 per cent, emotional factors block or hinder their tapping work, but with skill and a variety of tapping techniques that are beyond the scope of this book, it's possible to achieve good results. A small number of people don't respond well to EFT. One reason could be that they're using antidepressants or other types of medication that are known to suppress feelings.

If you feel EFT isn't working well for you, check out the Troubleshooting chapter on page 259. If you're still struggling you may find it easier to identify and release the blocks and achieve great results with the help of an EFT practitioner, or by attending an EFT training course. There are details of practitioners and training courses in the Further resources section on page 275.

There are several possible reasons that people can fall into this category, including having strongly-suppressed memories or emotional numbness, being unable to access emotions, and being in the fight/flight/freeze state. In this last case, the last thing a body is open to is healing. It just has to protect itself and survive, which can prevent any healing modality, conventional or alternative, working effectively. This doesn't mean that tapping won't work for you, but it could mean you don't get immediate results and need to be persistent.

Are you a control freak or a perfectionist?

If you're a control freak or a perfectionist – and I know there are a lot of us around! – sometimes the mind can go into overdrive and try to take over. With EFT it's very important to try to let go of your mind chatter as much as possible. Your mind may tell you that EFT can't or won't work, that it can't possibly make a difference, that it needs more information about how and why it could work. Sometimes reading some of the research (try googling 'EFT research') or some of the countless thousands of experiences others have had is enough to quieten the sceptical mind enough for it to allow you to give it a try.

If you can relate to this, check out the research on EFT in the Appendix page 281 and tap along to the tapping script for mums who don't believe in EFT in the Troubleshooting chapter on page 259.

Will it work if I'm sceptical about tapping?

Amazingly, yes! Being sceptical doesn't seem to prevent tapping from working well. However, some things that can block it from working include:

* not wanting it to work – ie you may (possibly unconsciously) have something to gain from it not working
* being pushed into using it by someone else when you yourself don't really want to feel different
* preferring to hold on to an issue rather than letting it go

Once you're aware of what's preventing you getting results there's often, though not always, a way into the process that will clear the blockage: see the Troubleshooting chapter on page 259 for some ideas.

Some mums spend a lot of time looking for solutions to their problems, often at night, and end up in a cycle of overthinking that leads to exhaustion and overwhelm. The mind finds it easier to identify solutions when it's calm and relaxed. The tapping scripts I offer in this book will help you calm your mind, so be open to being surprised at how new thoughts, ideas and inspirations pop into your head.

Remember you can refer to the Troubleshooting chapter on page 259 if you're not getting good results.

Self-sabotage, and how it can block any desired outcome

One of the most important things you need to know about, and which applies to any healing modality or positive intention, is self-sabotage (also known as resistance, inner objections, secondary gain, psychological reversal and polarity reversal). This is a state that blocks the path forward in a very concrete way. It can stop EFT in its tracks and block motivation, the realisation of specific goals and anything else you consciously want to achieve. Thankfully it's easy to neutralise the effect of this resistance. See the Troubleshooting chapter on page 259 for more on releasing self-sabotage.

The Quick-start Tapping Guide

Welcome to the Quick-Start Tapping Guide, which is designed to get you going with EFT in just a few minutes. If you've skipped the sections above and come straight here that's fine – just give it a go. If for any reason you've followed the procedure later on in this chapter and there's a chance that scepticism is preventing you giving this the attention it deserves – because it works exceedingly well most of the time – please read the sections above, which provide important background, first. This also applies if tapping isn't working very well for you. In particular, read the section titled Self-sabotage on page 269, and how it can block any desired outcome, and Will EFT work for me? on page 19, and if necessary, the Troubleshooting chapter on page 259.

The Tapping points

EFT involves tapping on points on the body with the fingertips to stimulate certain acupuncture points while tuning in to the problem. According to Gary Craig, the founder of EFT, negative emotions are caused by disruptions in the body's energy system. He bases this on his understanding of the Traditional Chinese Medicine system, which treats the channels of energy, or meridians, that run through the body. He says that when you feel a negative emotion such as anxiety or stress, the meridians become blocked, a bit like a hosepipe becoming kinked, and obstruct the flow of energy. Tapping on specific acupuncture points whilst deliberately focusing on the negative emotion or memory unblocks the meridian, allowing the energy to flow freely again. As you do this the upsetting emotions begin to dissipate. In short, tapping helps to restore the balance in the body's energy system.

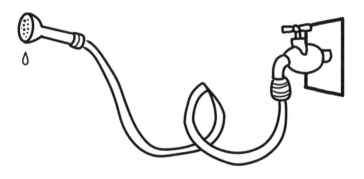

First, glance over the Tapping points description below, which illustrates the acupuncture points you'll be tapping on. You'll need this later as a reference.

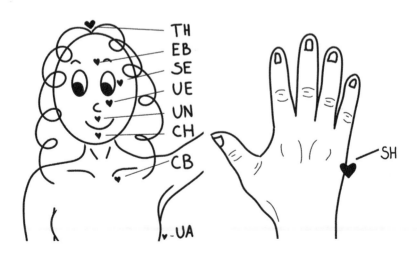

Side of Hand (SH): Along the outside edge of either hand. Use all the fingers of your other hand to tap on this point.

Top of Head (TH): Right on the top of the head, where you would balance a book. You can tap with all your fingers on and around this point.

Inside Eyebrow (EB): Where your eyebrow begins at the top of your nose. Use two fingers to make sure you hit the spot.

Side of Eye (SE): On the bone bordering the outside corner of the eye. Again, use two fingers.

Under Eye (UE): On the bone, directly under the eye socket.

Under Nose (UN): In the middle of the philtrum, the depression running from your nose to your mouth. Use one finger.

Chin (CH): In the centre of the dip below your bottom lip. Use one or more fingers.

Collarbone (CB): From the dip in your throat where your collarbones almost meet, go down two centimetres and outwards two centimetres (about an inch). This is the collarbone point. It should be just below your collarbone and just off your breastbone (the vertical bone in the centre of your chest). Use the whole palm of your hand here, and don't worry about getting the point exactly right as that will cover it.

Under Arm (UA): At the side of your body at the height of the bra strap (women) or parallel to the nipple (men). Use one or more fingers.

There's a script for the tapping routine that accompanies each daily challenge. If you want to make sure you're tapping correctly you can download a free demonstration video from Frazzledtofabulous. com/Bonus.

EFT process overview

Each round of EFT takes about five minutes, and that's all you need to do each day. A round starts with tapping on the outer side of your hand with the fingertips of the other (see the illustration on the next page). While tapping, you recite a statement three times, ideally aloud. You then tap on a sequence of points that are mainly on your face using the tips of one or more fingers. If you like you can imagine that your fingers are tapping a calming and peaceful colour of your choice into your body. It doesn't matter which hand you use to tap with or which side of your body you tap on – you can even use both hands on both sides at once. At the end of the round, put your hands, one over the other, in the centre of your chest and with a deep breath, say the word 'Transform'. This is a subconscious cue word, and many people find that it enhances the effect of the tapping.

The procedure is very simple. At first it will seem strange – because it *is* strange! You'll think 'How can this make any difference?' You may also think 'I'll look silly', so find a private place where you don't need to think about anything else. Distraction will affect the results. Approach this with an open mind, although if you feel sceptical that's fine. The procedure is very forgiving, and even if you get it wrong you'll likely get good results anyway. So if you're a perfectionist, relax. You're perfect just the way you are – and just the way you're not!

First, rate the intensity of your problem (eg overwhelmed, worried about your child, not feeling good enough, etc) on a scale from 0 (not a problem) to 10 (the most intense feeling you could have about it). If you are already at 0, chose another theme for the day or tap along to this one anyway, as you'll probably find it calming and may even relate to some of the tapping statements.

Now follow the instructions and tapping script for the day you are on in the 30-Day Challenge section of the book, tapping on each of the points in turn while saying, preferably aloud, the words or phrases beside each tapping point. So for instance for 'Chin: Releasing stress', tap on the chin point while saying 'Releasing stress'.

Once you've tapped on all the points repeating the statements in the tapping scripts for each day of the 30-Day Challenge, rate the intensity of the problem from 0 to 10 again. If you are at 0, great work! If not, and if you have time, repeat.

If the intensity hasn't gone down, read the Troubleshooting chapter on page 259.

Some people find it hard to rate the intensity of their problem with a number. If this is the case for you, you may like to rate it as a colour before and after tapping. As long as the colour changes, you know your relationship to the issue is evolving. If not, consult the Troubleshooting chapter on page 259. Alternatively you can rate the intensity by holding your hands apart in front of you to illustrate its size. As the intensity decreases, so will the distance between your hands.

PART 2
The Challenge

Introduction

Welcome to the Get Your Sanity Back 30-Day Challenge! I'm so excited you're here. I know that if you follow each of the instructions for the next 30 days you'll be setting strong foundations for permanent positive change for yourself and your children. I'm so happy that through this book you are embarking on this transformational journey and joining the hundreds of mums who have created fulfilling, loving and joyful lives for themselves and their families.

Why do the challenge?

You've bought the book. You want relief from stress, overwhelm and exhaustion, and from the anxiety of being a mother. It's not going to happen without taking action. Thirty days is a good amount of time to create a habit and lay the foundations of the life you want for yourself and your children. My wish for you is that tapping becomes as habitual as brushing your teeth. Once the habit's embedded, EFT will become your go-to place in times of stress, as in my story about using it with my mum at the A&E.

My intention for your 30-Day Challenge is that it will be a powerful, transformational practice and, most importantly, will give you a tool that you can use to embed good habits, create more calm in your life, enjoy your children more, and be more productive.

I ran this challenge online with a fabulous group of mums, whose feedback is included throughout this book so that you can see the incredible transformations they brought about for themselves and their children:

> 'When I started the challenge I had some reservations, mainly because of my lack of time. The biggest change is that I'm calmer with my child and husband and enjoy the present. I highly recommend that stressed mums enter the challenge. It's really simple, not time-consuming, and the results are awesome and beneficial for everybody surrounding you.' Elizabeth

Preparing for the challenge

Read the Quick Guide to EFT starting on page 14. If you're super-stressed and just want to get going you can skip this for now, but come back to it if you need more information about how to do the daily challenges.

1. Read the Disclaimer on page xvii.
2. Set your intention to commit to this challenge for the next 30 days, making the few minutes it takes more important than your to-do list, your sleep, your work, your home, and yes – even your family! I know these are strong words, but I know you want to change. Your children thrive when you're feeling good, and when they thrive you feel better.
3. As an optional extra to help you get the most from the challenge, buy the videos of the daily tapping scripts and visualisation at Frazzledtofabulous.com/Bonus. Reading them off the page works brilliantly but the videos bring them to life and can feel easier. Whether you want to buy the videos or not, pop along to this page to check out the free bonus materials.
4. I've designed the challenge to ideally start on a Monday so that you can have a rest or catch up every Sunday, but of course you can start whenever you want and use it however best suits your lifestyle.

5. Read only one daily chapter a day and take the specified action.
6. Find a journal you can use to track your progress or buy the Frazzled to Fabulous in 5 Minutes a Day Workbook from Frazzledtofabulous/Bonus

What if I miss a day?

If you miss a day, don't worry. Simply carry on from where you left off. If you're doing the challenge with other people you may want to skip the day you missed and move on so you can stay with them. If you feel stuck on a particular day, do a different day's challenge instead. If nothing inspires you, move on to the next day. The key is to continue and not give up. Read The Mum Who Fell Down the Hole on page 265 for more inspiration.

How the Challenge Works

Your daily minimum

Each day covers a different issue, and on most days there's a tapping script for the day which will take you about five minutes. On a few of the days you'll need a little extra time.

Your priority is to complete the daily tapping: you're establishing a new, useful, positive and stress-relieving habit. Make sure you commit to setting aside at least five minutes, six days a week, with a rest or catchup day. The challenge in this book sets Sundays as the rest day, but you can start the challenge any day of the week.

Create accountability and support

When you tell someone you're going to do something, you're much more likely to actually do it. The support and encouragement of that person or group of people increases your likely success rate even more. As a thank you for buying this book I invite you to join my private Facebook support group, where you can draw support from other mums engaging with this transformational challenge. Support for any change is important – I can assure you that doing this together, hearing about other mums' experiences and realising you're not the only one facing challenges, can make all the difference. It can be hard to make changes on your own, especially when the going gets tough as it may at times, so accountability and peer support will be there to encourage you every step of the way.

Part of the awesome feedback from mums doing this challenge was that they felt supported by others. Because they'd shared their intentions, they felt they have to follow through:

> 'What surprised me about the challenge was the warmth, support and friendships in the Facebook community.' Emma

If you don't feel comfortable joining the Facebook community that's okay: it's optional. You may want to keep what you're doing to yourself. If you're the sort of person who often starts something and doesn't finish it you may find that sharing your intentions and reading others' experiences this time will help you to succeed.

If Facebook isn't your thing but you do want to feel supported and accountable, why not gather a group of friends, school mums or book club members and do the challenge together, meeting weekly to share the answers to the questions from each day of the challenge and supporting one another.

If you feel the Facebook support group could be helpful you can access it at Frazzledtofabulous.com/Bonus, together with guidance on how to make the most of it.

Use the Troubleshooting chapter

If at any time you find yourself feeling too stressed, overwhelmed or exhausted to do the daily challenge or you've fallen behind and don't know how to get back into the daily routine, you'll find help and encouragement in the Troubleshooting chapter on page 259.

For extra motivation

I recommend keeping track of the changes you experience, and to make this easy I've created a Frazzled to Fabulous in 5 Minutes a Day Workbook which is available to download from Frazzledtofabulous. com/Bonus. Alternatively you can keep a journal and track your changes and experiences there. Completing this page every day or every week will help you see the impact of your daily tapping.

> 'This challenge has been such a wonderful experience, making tapping part of my daily routine – I am so keen to carry on. It's been really useful to highlight the core issues causing my problems and to make some inroads into releasing them and releasing the symptoms – and to find myself using them in the moment (aka when it all goes pear-shaped!) and more consistently with the children. Overall there has been an increase in my energy and my joy and my playfulness. I look forward to deepening my connection with myself! My husband and my children. Oh, and also releasing my sense and need for/of perfection.' Sarah-Jane

Charlotte's story

How EFT helped newly single mum

With my two young children I 'escaped' an unhealthy relationship. I was under police protection and it was a traumatic time. Being a newly single and working mother of a two-year-old and a three-month-old and suffering post-traumatic stress, this situation was more than just challenging.

I knew about EFT and the thought kept coming to me to do it, but I repeatedly told myself there was no time for me to tap, that the children's needs came first. Then those horrible moments of overwhelm would wash over me like a great wave of negativity and I thought I was literally going to crack. I'd feel so many emotions – hopelessness, guilt and anxiety. And even though I knew deep down that my response to situations creates the outcome, I still felt like a victim and that life had let me down.

I recall how I watched my babies sleeping one evening, saw how beautiful and precious they were. I knew in my heart I had the power to shift my perception and look for the gift in this situation; I could embrace the opportunity and grow, or break down and leave my children with no mother.

So I made my decision and the tapping process began…

Even the very first EFT routine felt like a relief and a victory. And there were actually plenty of windows of time to tap away negative thoughts and feelings that surfaced. Every short routine got me a little bit further along my journey of recovery.

It's been over a year, and I'm in a completely different place emotionally. I do at least three EFT routines every day.

Life feels wonderful now. I actually love my life as a single mum. I've my moments, of course, but I'm in control now and I just do EFT! Because I continue to give to myself through doing EFT, I have so much more to give my children. The metaphoric well is regularly filled up and so I share that with my children and am more inspired with life.

PART 3
Your Next 30 Days

Day 1

Are you headed for Destination Chaos?
Setting yourself up for success

'With tapping, I'm creating a daily habit to release stress and other negative emotions and to start creating more calm and ease in my own and my son's life. It feels empowering, miraculous, uplifting, comforting to be able to shift my state in just five minutes, and it's great to have an easy, portable tool that works. Since doing the challenge my partner has definitely noticed I'm more positive, calmer and more proactive, and family life just feels better. I've been feeling more confident and calm and in control of my own life. I'm feeling more able to stand up for myself in different situations. I'm using patience more rather than instantly reacting to situations, and I've felt excited to wake up for the first time in ages.' Laurie

Imagine you're a ship called *Mum* sailing in the ocean of life heading for Destination Chaos. When a ship changes course by even a tiny bit she completely changes her destination. This challenge is a navigation changer! It has the ability to lay the foundations for changing your course from Destination Chaos to Destination Calm, and all you have to do is show up every day for the next 30 days and follow the instructions.

Daily practice is important because your ship is sailing on the ocean surrounded by currents called:

❋ too much to do
❋ not enough time
❋ hamster wheel
❋ juggling too many balls
❋ my child won't wear his coat!

and more, all of which are pulling you back towards Destination Chaos. So it's essential to make doing this challenge more important than your to-do list and all the other currents in order to stay on course for Destination Calm! It only takes a minimum of five minutes of the 1440 available to you each day.

The best time to do your tapping is first thing in the morning, setting your course for Destination Calm at the start of the day and making it harder for your ship to veer off course. Setting your alarm to ring a few minutes earlier than usual to make time for yourself without the children would be ideal, although I know this may simply not be realistic for many of you whose children sleep with you/wake up before you/wake up when the alarm goes off, etc, in which case the

best time may be when your child is having a nap or at school. Some mums I know lock themselves in the loo for five minutes. Others tap in the car when they arrive at work.

You might prefer to tap last thing before bed, but please make sure it actually happens and you don't find yourself too tired to do anything extra! Doing it before bed can help you sleep better.

Consider how you'll be able to fit the challenge in at weekends and during any holidays or school breaks that involve a change to your normal routine. It may be that you can do it at a certain time on most days, while on others you're busy at that time. If that's the case, think ahead about those unusual days and decide in advance when you'll be able to make that special time for yourself to create change for you and your family.

I feel too overwhelmed by my to-do list to think about this

If you this is you, don't worry. Simply do what you can in the time you have. Doing something is better than doing nothing, and I don't want resistance to planning to stop you from doing the actual challenge!

I'm not a planner

That's okay! If you're a mum who doesn't like planning or controlling her day, simply do the tapping exercises when it feels right or when you can fit them in. The key is to actually do them rather than not do them, so whatever way works for you is the right way.

Action

1. Put the times you plan to do your challenges into your diary or calendar. Consider the best times at weekends, in the school holidays and on other days that follow a different rhythm. Each day the challenge will probably take at least five and at most fifteen minutes, ideally at the start of the day so that you begin your day well.

2. If you're using the Facebook support group for support, you'll want a few minutes later in the day to read the posts of other mums in your Facebook tribe and comment supportively – just a couple of words is all that's necessary – helping each other to stay on track and complete the 30 days easily.

3. Remember, if you want to change you'll have to do things differently, making these actions more important than your to-do list or your exhaustion. Your children will start reaping the benefits of having a happier mum! If it ever feels overwhelming, just do what you can with the time you have; anything is better than nothing.

4. Think of one thing you're grateful for today and bask in your appreciation of it for a few moments. Even when life feels like the pits there's always at least one thing to be grateful for in the moment; for example having fresh air to breathe, knowing that you and your children are safe and away from war zones, seeing the sunset, noticing your child's eyes light up.

Optional Extras for Maximum Benefit

5. Do one small, practical and manageable thing today to ease one of the things that stressed you out during the day.

6. Write down your reflections in your journal or in the Frazzled to Fabulous in 5 Minutes a Day Workbook that you can buy at Frazzledtofabulous.com/Bonus.

7. Accountability and support: If you're doing this with a friend or group of friends, share with them when you're intending to do the daily challenge and one thing you're grateful for today. If you're doing it on your own and feel you would benefit from accountability and support, I strongly encourage you to hop into the Facebook support group, also accessible from Frazzledtofabulous.com/Bonus. Read a few comments from the other mums and share some encouragement, support or inspiration to help you and your tribe members stay on track.

Day 2

De-stress

'I was babysitting my brother, who wouldn't fall asleep because our mum was out – he was getting all upset so I decided to try tapping with him. He was very suspicious, but he mumbled the words along with me (under the blanket so I wouldn't see!) and let me tap on him – he was asleep about five minutes later.'
Abigail

Despite all the challenges you face in your life as a mum, you're already on Day 2. You're setting a new course for your ship towards Destination Calm!

And I want to celebrate that – I'm doing my happy dance!

How did you get on yesterday? Were you able to see how you could carve out a few minutes each day? If not, don't worry – you're here today, and that's amazing.

This challenge is about making changes in your life, and you're here because you want to do that. You may be thinking 'Yes, but how, when I've too much to do/lots of children/the school runs/ work/elderly parents to look after/illness/an unhelpful partner/no partner' etc. The number of times I've heard 'It's just the way it is... (sigh)'.

And yet something inside you *knows* life can't go on the way it is: not for you, and not for your family.

Action

1. Today's exercise is the SOS process. It's probably the most important process you'll do in this Challenge. It's perfect for when you're feeling so stressed and frazzled you can't think straight. It's very simple: all you do is put your hands in the centre of your chest and take at least three deep slow breaths. That's it! If you have time, repeat until you feel calmer and more relaxed. Do this several times a day. Before each deep breath say 'De-stress' or 'Releasing this stress,' whichever feels more comfortable. I would love you to do this every time you feel your stress levels rise, today and over the remaining days of the Challenge. Some mums set a timer to remind them to do it every hour. Others like to do it when they're in the shower or every time they go to the loo so it doesn't take up any extra time. You could put a little reminder note in your purse, in the toilet or in your office – wherever you'll see it often. You can also download a reminder tapping image and a video of a full round of de-stress tapping from Frazzledtofabulous.com/Bonus.
2. Think about one thing that you're grateful for today and bask in your appreciation of it for a few moments.

Optional Extras for Maximum Benefit

3. Do one small, practical and manageable thing today to ease one of the things that stressed you out during the day.
4. Write down your reflections in your journal or in the Frazzled to Fabulous in 5 Minutes a Day Workbook that you can buy at Frazzledtofabulous.com/Bonus.
5. Describe to the other mums in the Facebook support group how you got on with the breathing exercise in stressful moments today. Please follow the instructions on the page Frazzledtofabulous.com/Bonus about where you can leave your

feedback about your Day 2 challenge. Read a few comments from other mums in the Facebook support group and share some encouragement, support or inspiration to help you and your tribe members stay on track.

Day 3

What are the consequences of **not** changing?

'Nearly everything on the list of negative emotions was above an 8! But the top one is stress and not having enough time. I get impatient, lose my temper, shout at my children and husband and end up blaming everyone else. I look forward to moving beyond this!' Katie

The above feedback is from a mum after she'd completed Day 3. Today's task is to take stock of your emotions at the start of the 30-day challenge. If you find yourself struggling, use the Facebook support group as a source of encouragement and inspiration. You can access it from Frazzledtofabulous.com/Bonus.

Up to now you've had no time to change, or you may have tried to change without success. Perhaps you hadn't even realised that things could be different.

Well – what would the consequences of not taking action right now be?

Are things going to get better all on their own?

Are you waiting till your children have grown up?

Are you waiting for a blue moon?

Wouldn't you like to look back a month from now and say 'I'm so glad I finally took that step to change my life!'?

Over these 30 days you are going to be learning to use EFT and putting the foundations in place to create permanent changes in your life that will result in your having more time, more energy, more fun and patience with your children, and more productivity.

The only time you really have is now. How are you going to make the most of this and every moment? The choices you make today will affect your future. Imagine a time ahead when you feel calm, clear and relaxed and are enjoying your children. Taking action in the present, right *now*, towards those goals can make this happen. Saying 'I haven't got the time' won't. I've helped a lot of people move beyond this time obstacle.

So what are the consequences of not changing?

Today we're going to take a look at the negative feelings, thoughts and behaviours that are creating the stressful life you're experiencing.

Action

1. In the My Biggest Challenges questionnaire on the next page, rate the intensity of the listed emotions, challenges and thoughts on a scale from 0 to 10, where 0 means it doesn't affect you at all and 10 is the greatest possible intensity. You can complete the questionnaire on the next page or in the Frazzled to Fabulous in 5 Minutes a Day Workbook (purchasable at Frazzledtofabulous. com/Bonus. These symptoms are the top challenges as surveyed by the mums who have taken my online challenge.

2. Complete the 'What's the cost of not changing?' form on page 54 or in the workbook.

Optional Extras for Maximum Benefit

3. Think of one thing you're grateful for today and bask in your appreciation of it for a few moments.

4. Do one small, practical and manageable thing today to ease one of your challenges.

5. Write down your reflections in your journal or the Frazzled to Fabulous in 5 Minutes a Day Workbook.

6. Share with your Facebook support group
   ❋ what themes stood out for you when completing the questionnaire
   ❋ what action you're going to take today to ease one of your challenges
   ❋ one thing you're grateful for

7. Read a few of the other mums' comments and share some encouragement, support or inspiration yourself to help you all stay on track.

My Biggest Challenges questionnaire

Symptom	Rating (0-10)	Symptom	Rating (0-10)
Emotion		**Behaviour**	
Anger		Beating myself up for not saying NO	
Anxiety		Cravings – sugar, coffee, wine, cigarettes, etc	
Exhaustion		Letting people down	
Fear		Overcommitting	
Guilt		Not putting myself first	
Overthinking		There's always something more important than me	
Overwhelm		**Health challenges**	
Procrastination		Digestive problems	
Resentment		Headaches/migraines	
Stress		Period problems	
Add your own particular challenges here		Trouble sleeping	

What's the cost of not changing?

To yourself?

To your children?

To your partner?

To your home?

To your work?

To your health?

To your finances?

I know it's a long list, and some mums have told me they found filling in this questionnaire an uncomfortable experience. If that's the case for you, please don't worry! We'll start releasing these uncomfortable feelings tomorrow.

However, I don't want you to have to hold on to any stress created as a result of completing the questionnaire, so if you can't wait until tomorrow either repeat yesterday's de-stress challenge, especially if you don't have much time, or go straight on to Day 4, where you'll be releasing the upsetting feelings you've rated today. If you haven't got time right now, simply imagine or visualise that you're putting all those uncomfortable feelings into a box with a secure lid, where you can leave them for now and address them tomorrow. And don't give up – it's going to get easier!

Day 4

Your top challenge

'I'd never done EFT before and at first I wasn't entirely sure what it was going to do for me, but it was easy and quick to do and each time, afterwards I felt more 'at one'. Knowing that overwhelm, anxiety and waking up at night with the 'to-do list' buzzing in my head are experienced by many others, not just me, and that someone (Tamara) understands that. It just makes you feel better, more able to deal with things in a positive way and not stress about the little things.' Vicky

You're back for more, and I'm so happy for you!

This challenge is about making changes in your life, and you're here because you want to change! You may be thinking 'Yes, but how, when I have too much to do, lots of children, school runs, work, elderly parents to look after, illness, an unhelpful partner/no partner' and so on! The number of times I've heard 'It's just the way it is'... sigh...

And yet something inside you knows life can't go on the way it is: not for you, and not for your family.

We're going to jump into tapping to release some of that pressure.

Before we get going, please read the Disclaimer on page xvii.

Today is your first tapping experience on this challenge. If you haven't done EFT before, read the Quick Guide to EFT starting on page 14. If you're too stressed right now to take on any new information and just want to get going, that's okay, but if you find you have any questions do go back and read that chapter. If you're a more visual person you can download a free how-to-tap video from Frazzledtofabulous.com/Bonus.

And now for today's challenge: we're going to tap on the top issue that you listed in response to Day 3's question 'What are the consequences of *not* changing?'

I asked you to rate your own experiences of my clients' most common symptoms.

You may be interested to know that when I ran this challenge online, at the beginning of the challenge the mums' ratings for overwhelm, stress, guilt, overthinking, and 'how am I going to get it all done?' averaged 8 or more out of 10.

Today I would like you to bring your biggest challenge from yesterday's list to mind and answer the following questions as you think about it:

❀ What emotions does the challenge bring up in you? For instance, you might feel frustrated, fearful, panicky, inadequate, sad, anxious, etc; or use your own words for your feelings if they feel more relevant. If the challenge brings up more than one emotion, write them all down and choose the most intense one for now

❀ Where do you feel the challenge and its emotions in your body?

❀ What is the physical sensation in that part of your body? For example it might be tension, pressure, butterflies, an ache, emptiness, etc. If you find it hard to answer these questions allow yourself to guess, or take the first answer that pops up

Putting your answers to the questions above together might produce, for example, 'anxiety and butterflies in my stomach', or 'tension and stress in my shoulders', 'fear and pressure in my chest', or something else.

Now that you've identified the emotion, where you feel it in your body and the physical sensation, let's get tapping to release it.

If you have more than one challenge with the same intensity, repeat today's tapping script for each one or as many as you have time for. You can come back to this during the 30-Day Challenge whenever you're feeling strong emotions that you're not coping with. It only takes five minutes to make a difference!

Action

1. Rate the intensity of your top challenge or the emotion associated with it from 0 to 10, where 0 isn't affecting you at all and 10 is maximum intensity.
2. Follow the tapping script on page 61. Feel free to change the words to describe how you're feeling more accurately.
3. After tapping, rate the intensity of your top challenge again from 0 to 10.
4. If it hasn't gone down at all, check the Troubleshooting chapter on page 259 to find out what you can do next.
5. Think of one thing you're grateful for today and bask in your appreciation of it for a few moments.

Optional Extras for Maximum Benefit

6. Repeat the tapping script as many times as you have time for (and remember, just once is better than never!) with the aim of reducing the intensity to 0.
7. Take one small, manageable and practical action today to address this challenge.
8. Write down your reflections in your journal or the Frazzled to Fabulous in 5 Minutes a Day Workbook.
9. Follow the instructions at Frazzledtofabulous.com/Bonus about where to leave your feedback in the Facebook support group and share:
   ❀ how your relationship with your top challenge is changing as a result of tapping
   ❀ what action you're going to take today to address your top challenge
   ❀ one thing you are grateful for

10. Read a few comments from the other mums and share some encouragement, support or inspiration to help you and your tribe members stay on track.

Day 4: Your top challenge – tapping script

Side of hand:	Even though this [state your top challenge] is all-consuming and it's preventing me seeing clearly, I acknowledge that this is where I am right now. Even though I have this [top challenge], it makes me feel [emotion] and it's stopping me having peace in my life, I accept myself and the challenge. Even though I'm used to this [top challenge] I really want to get over it, and I choose to know that it's possible to change.
Top of head:	This [emotion] about this [top challenge]. [For example 'This sadness about not putting myself first.']
Eyebrow:	I can feel it in my [state part of body, or guess if you can't identify it].
Side of eye:	I'm noticing the way it makes my body feel.
Under eye:	This [top challenge] is stopping me being free.
Under nose:	This [top challenge] is stopping me moving forwards.
Chin:	This [top challenge] is stopping me having the life I want.
Collarbone:	This [top challenge] is affecting my family too.
Under arm:	I can't see a way out right now.
Top of head:	My mind is telling me there's no way out.
Eyebrow:	I'm open to the possibility of letting go of the need to know how to release my feelings about this [top challenge].
Side of eye:	Maybe this challenge has been with me a long time.

Under eye:	Maybe from childhood or even earlier.
Under nose:	Maybe my parents also suffer/suffered with this challenge.
Chin:	Maybe I learnt it from them.
Collarbone:	But the buck stops with me.
Under arm:	I'm not going to pass this on to my children.
Top of head:	Tapping helps me release this challenge.
Eyebrow:	The more I release it, the freer I become.
Side of eye:	The more I release it, the freer my children become.
Under eye:	By releasing more of this [top challenge] I can breathe more freely.
Under nose:	I'm open to feeling softer and more relaxed.
Chin:	I'm open to trusting that there's a solution to this [top challenge].
Collarbone:	I choose to infuse calm and ease into my life and this [top challenge].
Under arm:	I choose to have compassion and to accept my current situation.
Chest:	[taking a deep breath] Transform.

How did you get on with what may have been your first tapping experience?

If you're feeling more peaceful, lighter, tingly, more relaxed, more energised or more tired these are signs that the EFT has caused a shift. Other signs include yawning and burping. If you're feeling more tired, it's a good thing! It means you're starting to release some of the stress you've been holding in your body all this time. Drink lots of water today and try to get an early night.

If you're experiencing no difference in yourself or feeling worse, go to the Troubleshooting chapter on page 259 for your next steps.

If you'd like to do the daily tapping along with me you can buy the videos at Frazzledtofabulous.com/Bonus; they're especially helpful if you're a visual learner.

Day 5

I can't change!

'Tapped with my youngest this morning because she was a bit upset as her big sis wasn't going into school today – I asked her what she was feeling and she said 'jealous' and 'most times I want to go to school but sometimes I don't', so I tapped on that for her ♡. Her jealous feeling went from a 10 to a 3 first round and then down to 'it's gone and I can't feel anything', and she then said 'I want to feel excited' so we tapped on that for just one round and she was 'up and at em'.' Sophie

Today is all about change and your fear of and resistance to it. You're reading this book because you want to change. The good news is that by following the instructions in this book you're taking five minutes every day to create a new habit. This new habit of tapping will begin to release the stress that's been keeping you from being able to think straight and see how your life can be easier and more harmonious.

Yesterday was your first day of proper tapping. How did you get on?

Here are some comments I've received from clients taking my online challenge after their first day of tapping:

'Afterwards I felt exhilarated and ready to face the day. Am excited and looking forward to making a much needed change in my life.'

'As the EFT went on I found I was becoming more and more relaxed, less irritated.'

'Tapping has made me feel immediately uplifted and energised.'

If you don't feel any relief from the feelings associated with your challenge after tapping, there are lots of tips for improving your results in the Troubleshooting chapter on page 259.

Today's tapping routine is quite playful. The script includes some phrases that may not ring true for you, but try them on for size anyway. This way of tapping is really about shaking up your thoughts and feelings: it might feel a bit confusing but I encourage you to go with it. It's a bit like emptying the contents of a messy cupboard onto the floor before you can start to create order from them, which we'll start doing soon!

Action

1. Rate the level of your belief that you can't change on a scale of 0 to 10, where 0 means you don't believe you can change at all and 10 means you totally believe you can. If you can't relate to this issue choose a script from another day that's more relevant to how you're feeling.

2. Follow the tapping script on the next page. Feel free to change my words to describe how you're feeling more accurately.

3. After tapping, rate your level of belief that you can't change again on the same scale.

4. If it hasn't gone down, check the Troubleshooting chapter on page 265 to find out what to do next.

5. Think of one thing you're grateful for today and bask in your appreciation of it for a few moments.

Optional Extras for Maximum Benefit

6. Repeat the tapping script as many times as you have time for (and remember, once is better than never!) with the aim of reducing the intensity to 0.

7. Do one small, practical and manageable thing today to create positive change for yourself.

8. Write down your reflections in your journal or workbook.

9. Share with the Facebook support group on Frazzledtofabulous. com/Bonus:
   * how you feel about the possibility of changing, and what came up for you during the tapping
   * what action you're going to take today to create change for yourself
   * one thing you're grateful for

10. Read a few comments from the other mums and share some encouragement, support or inspiration to help you and your tribe members stay on track.

Day 5: I can't change! – tapping script

Side of hand: Even though I can't change, I acknowledge that this is the way it is right now.
Even though I'm juggling so many balls and I'm scared that change might make my life harder before it gets easier, I accept myself and my situation.
Even though I've tried to change in the past but it hasn't lasted and I've given up, I choose to know that sustainable change is possible.

Top of head: I can't change.
Eyebrow: It's too difficult.
Side of eye: I've tried before and it hasn't worked.
Under eye: Part of me feels like giving up.
Under nose: Part of me knows I can't go on the way I am.
Chin: I'm juggling so many balls.
Collarbone: Not changing is affecting my health, my work and my family.
Under arm: I'm scared changing will make my life harder.

Top of head: I don't know what change would be like.
Eyebrow: Who would I be if I changed?
Side of eye: Part of me feels comfortable with what I know and what's familiar.
Under eye: This constant hamster wheel of life sometimes feels unbearable.
Under nose: I'm now allowing all these 'can't change' feelings to be here.
Chin: I'm noticing how my body feels right now, without judgement.
Collarbone: I'm noticing my feet on the floor.

Under arm:	I'm taking a fuller, deeper breath. [take a deep breath]
Top of head:	I'm open to the possibility of releasing the need to know how to change.
Eyebrow:	I choose to trust that I'm taking steps to create change right now.
Side of eye:	Maybe change could be easier than I think?
Under eye:	I'm open to the possibility of celebrating these few minutes for myself.
Under nose:	The more I can take care of my own needs, the easier it is to take care of others.
Chin:	I'm celebrating these few minutes that I've carved out for myself.
Collarbone:	I choose to start by giving myself five minutes every day.
Under arm:	I choose to know that big changes start with small steps.
Chest:	[taking a deep breath] Transform.

Day 6

Time? What time?

'Just did the tapping twice on having no time, and feel so calm now. I always feel like I don't have enough time, but now after the tapping I feel like I don't care about the to-do list – it's my life and I can choose what I put on the to-do list anyway! My real self knows this and tapping seems to bring me back to my real self. Before the tapping I was totally in my ego with the to-do list swirling around in my head.' Zoe

It's Day 6. Well done for showing up here again! I can see that you're really committed to creating positive change in your own and your children's lives, and I'm so pleased you haven't given up.

These are a few of the messages left on the Facebook support group page after the first two days of tapping on a previous online challenge:

'I never experienced tapping before and I can't believe that after a whole day of feeling that I could hardly keep my eyes open I'm now feeling completely relaxed, no usual evening back pain, and energised.'

'Having had an exhausting night waking up with my daughter the tapping actually instantly made me feel energised.'

'Well, that worked. I felt quite amazing and relaxed after that … even though my to-do list is bonkers, it feels achievable…'

It's really important to me that you have a good experience. So if you aren't, please read the Troubleshooting chapter on page 259.

Today's tapping is all about time.

So many mums I speak to say they don't have enough time for everything they have to do. But you've carved out this moment to read this chapter, and I want to really acknowledge that. On Day 11 I talked about carving out time for yourself every day, and I know this can be a real stumbling block for many mums. So I want to address it further.

Until now it's likely that you've had no time or very little time: you may have tried to change and perhaps succeeded for a while, and then fallen back into old patterns. Maybe you know that change is needed but you don't know how to start. Maybe you're wondering whether this is the right time for this challenge – because you don't have time!

Knowing that you need to make changes but haven't got the time to do this can feel like being in a pressure cooker. This can lead to stress, overwhelm, sleeplessness and exhaustion. So here are your actions for today.

Action

1. Rate your belief that you don't have enough time for everything you have to do from 0 to 10, where at 0 you don't believe it at all and at 10 you totally believe it. If you can't relate to this issue choose a script from another day that's more relevant to how you're feeling.

2. Follow the tapping script on the next page. Feel free to change my words to describe how you're feeling more accurately.

3. Rate your belief again that you don't have enough time for everything you have to do on the scale of 0 to 10.

4. If your rating hasn't gone down, check the Troubleshooting chapter on page 259 to find out what to do next.

5. Think of one thing you're grateful for today and bask in your appreciation of it for a few moments.

Optional Extras for Maximum Benefit

6. Repeat the tapping script as many times as you have time for (and once is better than never!) with the aim of reducing the intensity to 0.

7. Do one small, practical and manageable thing today to create more time for yourself.

8. Write down your reflections in your journal or workbook.

9. Share with the Facebook support group:
    * your relationship with time, and what came up for you during the tapping
    * what action you're going to take today to create more time for yourself
    * one thing you're grateful for

10. Read a few of the comments from the other mums and share some encouragement, support or inspiration to help you and your tribe members stay on track.

Day 6: Time? What time? – tapping script

Side of hand: Even though I've haven't even got time to breathe, I acknowledge myself and the effort I'm making.
Even though mums don't have time – it's just the way it is and I have to keep going – I accept myself and my situation.
Even though I don't have a good relationship with time yet, I'm open to the possibility of this changing.

Top of head: Sometimes it feels like I've got no time.
Eyebrow: There's so much to do that I don't even know where to start.
Side of eye: I end up doing nothing productive at all.
Under eye: It's hard to prioritise my time.
Under nose: I end up procrastinating and then all the time is wasted.
Chin: Sometimes I wonder what I did with my time before I had children.
Collarbone: My relationship with time stresses me out.
Under arm: Seven days in a week is not enough.

Top of head: If only there were 30 hours a day or 8 days a week!
Eyebrow: I could so use that extra time.
Side of eye: This lack of time makes me feel overwhelmed.
Under eye: I'm open to the possibility of letting a little bit of this overwhelm go.
Under nose: I have THIS moment.
Chin: I have set aside these five minutes to do EFT.
Collarbone: I'm open to the possibility of acknowledging the time that I *have* carved out for myself.

Under arm:	I choose to celebrate *these* five minutes that I'm using to change my relationship with time.
Top of head:	I wonder what life would be like if I carved out five minutes for EFT every day to release my stress.
Eyebrow:	EFT will help me manage my time with more clarity, calm and focus.
Side of eye:	I'm open to the possibility of infusing the time I do have with more ease and trust.
Under eye:	I choose to be curious about my relationship with time.
Under nose:	Maybe time could become my friend.
Chin:	Maybe I can accept this moment just as it is.
Collarbone:	Maybe I can release my judgement about my relationship with time.
Under arm:	I choose to create a positive relationship with time.
Chest:	[taking a deep breath] Transform.

Harriet's story

EFT has transformed this mum's experience of parenting

Harriet was introduced to EFT after experiencing flashbacks following a miscarriage. Since then she has used it for a subsequent birth trauma, and since taking part in the 30-Day Tapping Challenge she now uses it daily to release stress and as a parenting tool. Harriet found that the sense of community created in the online support group, which is an integral part of the challenge, helped her to stay focused and committed to tapping every day. She encouraged her friends to take part too, and had encouraging chats with them at the school gate about how they were getting on. The big take-home message for her is the importance of self-care. Even when she didn't have much time as a busy mum, she found that five minutes of tapping could make all the difference.

Before she started tapping she hadn't noticed that her default position was stressing about everything. Her constant thoughts of 'I'm going to fail', 'I'm not going to be good enough', or 'It's going to be difficult' are now in the past. She was also, like many mums in our culture, carrying a lot of beliefs such as 'I should be able to be an energetic supermum who can keep all the plates spinning' and 'I need to create amazing experiences for my children'. She would read all the parenting books to find solutions to parenting problems arising such as potty training and weaning, only to get more stressed because they all offered different solutions.

Harriet has been tapping regularly for a number of years now, and through tapping has managed to release the pressure she put upon herself. She recalls that while it hasn't been easy, it's been very worthwhile for both her and her children. When stress arises now she's become skilled at noticing the challenging thoughts or feelings and nipping them in the bud with EFT. She just taps on the problem and allows her own parenting truth to arise, and she now feels massively more optimistic. She's very pragmatic about her parenting and knows that there'll be days when she feels she's messed up or loses her temper. When that happens, she knows how to recentre herself quickly using EFT, knowing that she's doing her best and that that is good enough.

Day 7

Catch up and recap

'Just had such a wonderful tapping experience with my 15-year-old son. He starts his end-of-year exams tomorrow. They are a really big deal. He's worked hard for the last few weeks revising. He confided tonight that he is super stressed and anxious. He said he'd like to do some tapping. The intensity of his anxiety was 9 out of 10. When we finished, it was at 0. All his initial fears of failing and not having done enough revision were dispelled. I then tested him on 15 difficult questions and he nailed it! He said 'The tapping has helped me focus, and know I can do it'.' Catherine

You'll be pleased to know that today is a catch-up day! You've worked really hard this week, so big congratulations for showing up every day and starting to create positive change for yourself and your family.

This week you started by carving out a five-minute slot in your day to create an opening during which you can start releasing your stress and overwhelm. I know this isn't easy and that there may have been days when it simply wasn't possible, and that's okay. The key is not to beat yourself up or feel like a failure because you couldn't do it. When you're creating a new habit it's hard to make it happen every day. Most people brush their teeth whatever else is going on in the lives, sometimes even more than twice a day. Once your daily tapping is a habit you won't even have to make an effort: once instilled, it'll just happen, like brushing your teeth!

That's why we have catch-up days built into this programme. If you've fallen behind you can use today to catch up, or you can have a rest and simply start again tomorrow where you left off.

If you're up to date, do a happy dance, or repeat one of the previous days.

On Day 2 I taught you one of the most important methods for de-stressing, which takes under 30 seconds (you can give it longer if you have more time) and is useful if you're feeling too stressed to do a full round of tapping. Simply put your hands in the centre of your chest and take three or more slow breaths, optionally saying 'De-stress' or 'Releasing this stress'.

Day 3 was a challenging day when I asked you to take stock of your life right now and of the emotions, thoughts and behaviours that occupy most of your time and energy.

On Days 4 to 6 you began tapping in earnest: on not being able to change; on having no time; and then on starting to address the biggest challenge revealed by the questionnaire – all probably your biggest reasons for picking this book up in the first place.

Next week we'll continue to chip away at these challenges that life presents, and I'll introduce some EFT for visualising your most Blissful Day.

Action

1. If you're up to speed and want to do some more tapping to create more momentum, you can repeat one of the tapping scripts from previous days or simply have a rest day.
2. If you feel you'd benefit from seeing tapping in action, check out the Frazzled to Fabulous Membership Club at Frazzledtofabulous. com/Bonus.
3. Do something for yourself, something with your children, and something with your partner, relatives or friends. This might look like a big ask, but think small: it can take just a few minutes, or more if you have it. For example, you could look in the mirror and tell yourself that you're doing a great job; you could give your children a big hug; and you could look into the eyes of your partner and tell them that you love them.

Day 8

Creating your Blissful Day: Part 1

'I just did the 'Blissful Day' visualisation and wow it was amazing. I connected to lots of emotions like joy, pride, satisfaction, happiness, and had some tingles going around my head. I used to practise gratitude intensively and experience the same feeling of openness and love. Thank you, Tamara, today I am grateful for your work.' Erika

Congratulations! You're back for your second week to continue your adventure, and I'm so happy for you!

For today's challenge, read the visualisation for creating your Blissful Day. Let your imagination flow – dream big and be playful. Imagine you could wave a magic wand and create a magical, Blissful Day for yourself, even if it's unrealistic. Tomorrow we'll tap on the energy and the qualities of that day to increase your sense of wellbeing, and we'll revisit this regularly. As an optional extra, I encourage you to revisit your Blissful Day scene or image every day. When the going gets tough you can remind yourself of the image of what you want and how it will make you feel.

Some mums doing the online challenge reported being unable to imagine achieving their Blissful Day. Here is some great feedback that explains how this visualisation helps:

'My initial thoughts today were that there was no way I could achieve my Blissful Day, given that I'm working all day/night,

but as I got going I realised that having a sense of feeling my Blissful Day was all I needed to get me through. I began to feel lighter and more fluid as I reached the end.' Brindi

Action

Make sure you won't be disturbed so that you can fully immerse yourself in this process.

1. Read the visualisation on page 85 for creating your Blissful Day, even if you can't see yourself achieving it as your life stands right now, or by the end of the 30 days, or even ever. I'm asking you to do this so that you have a positive image to focus on. I invite you to dream big and be playful. Imagine that you can wave a magic wand and create a Blissful Day for yourself, and then when the going gets tough you can remind yourself of the image you created in your mind and how it makes you feel. You can even record yourself reading the visualisation on page 85 out loud so that you can listen to it with your eyes closed. A recorded version is included in the subscription to the Frazzled to Fabulous Membership Club's daily videos at Frazzledtofabulous.com/Bonus.

2. Write down/type out/make notes on/draw/create your Blissful Day. Make sure it's short enough for you to be willing to read over it daily. Keep it where you'll see it every day, perhaps on the wall in the loo, on your phone, on the door of the cupboard where you keep your morning tea or coffee, or by your bed. Even if brief notes are all you have time for, that's good enough.

3. You may even choose to create a vision board. This visualisation tool involves creating a collage of words and pictures that represent your goals and dreams on some kind of background. It could be a board or a wall, or you could even store them as a specific collection on your phone. Use this creative process to set your intentions about what you want in your life. Looking at it should make you feel good. Keep it somewhere that you will see it often, such as by your desk, in your bedroom, or as your screensaver. Creating and maintaining a vision board is one of

the powerful exercises recommended in the popular book *The Secret*, and there are many more in Abraham-Hicks' *Ask And It Is Given*, which describes how to intentionally apply the Law of Attraction to bring about what you want. It's also a fun activity to do with your children. My daughter and I have spent many New Year's Days sitting on the floor surrounded by magazines, scissors and glue, listening to music and creating our intentions for the new year.

4. Think of one thing that you're grateful for today and bask in your appreciation of it for a few moments.

Optional Extras for Maximum Benefit

5. Do one small, practical and manageable thing today to move towards creating your Blissful Day.
6. Write down your reflections in your journal or workbook.
7. Share with the Facebook support group:
   * how visualising your Blissful Day makes you feel
   * what action you're going to take today to move towards creating your Blissful Day
   * one thing you're grateful for
8. Read a few comments from the other mums and share some encouragement, support or inspiration to help you and your tribe members stay on track.

Throughout the Challenge I'll be encouraging you to focus on the feelings that arise as you imagine your Blissful Day, to keep that blissful energy alive in you.

Day 8: Visualisation

Imagine that you can wave a magic wand and have the Blissful Day of your dreams, even if you don't know how this could happen.

Imagine, visualise, or get a sense of yourself waking up in the morning of your Blissful Day, having slept really well and feeling filled with excitement. Breathe that excitement into every cell of your body as you think about all the things you're looking forward to today.

How are you going to start your day? Breakfast in bed? Meditation? Going out for a run? A long bath? Fill the start of your day with things you love doing to set your navigation system, not just to Destination Calm but to Destination Blissful! You don't have to think about the practicalities – just tune into the kinds of things that lift your spirits. Know and trust that everything – your children, your home, your work, and any other responsibilities – is taken care of so that you can utterly relax into your Blissful Day.

Think about how you're going to spend your morning. Will you be with your children? Your partner? Alone? Are you taking time out for yourself? Are you doing things you love? Are you seeing friends? Just notice what possibilities really fill you with joy and excitement and breathe those feelings into every cell of your body.

Think about what you're going to do for lunch. Where are you eating? Who's making it? Who are you with? Fill that experience with joy, pleasure and ease. Take a deep breath.

Think about how you're going to spend the afternoon. Where are you? Who are you with? What are you doing? How are you feeling? Is it joy, love, freedom, pleasure, excitement, peace? Notice where you feel these feelings in your body and breathe them into every cell.

Think about your evening. Where are you? Who are you with? What are you eating? How are you spending the time before and after your meal? Fill these moments with joy, fun, magic, bliss, ease, calm, and any other feelings you want to experience, and breathe them into every cell of your body.

See yourself going to bed that night, lying in your warm cosy bed feeling so grateful, happy and relaxed after this amazing day, and allow yourself to drift into a gentle, peaceful sleep.

When you think about your whole day, make the delicious feelings bigger, bolder, brighter and more vivid, and fill your Blissful Day with more magic, miracles, pleasure, ease and peace. Breathe all of these wonderful feelings into every cell of your body.

Day 9

Creating your Blissful Day: Part 2

> *'Woohoo!! I've had amazing success with tapping today! I was SO angry about something, really incandescent, so I tapped to release it. Instead of anxiety, I actually felt something tilt inside me and it's gone! I just don't care about it anymore. I feel brilliant and ebullient.'* Rebecca

Today we're going do some EFT on yesterday's Blissful Day visualisation, to ground it in all the cells in your body.

Positive visualisation can increase your sense of joy, ease and happiness. I often start my day completing a journal called *The 15 Minute Miracle* (www.15minutemiracle.com) which includes, among other things, a section for imagining the life of your wildest dreams and then exploring manageable steps towards it. When I start my day doing things I love like tapping, meditating, running or going to the allotment I'm more productive, more in the flow, nicer to people, having more fun and moving towards my dreams!

Tapping on things that you want helps to raise your vibration and make you feel good. When you feel good, life flows better, you have more clarity and you feel happier and more positive. Each time you do this, you move closer to your Blissful Day!

Action

1. Think of the Blissful Day visualisation you created yesterday. Rate your level of positive emotion, eg joy, excitement, peace, happiness, on a scale from 0 to 10. This time 0 represents no joy (or other positive emotion you've selected) at all and 10, the most possible. In this case the tapping will increase your positive feelings rather than reducing your negative ones.
2. Follow the tapping script on the next page. Feel free to change my words to describe how you're feeling more accurately.
3. Focusing on your Blissful Day again, notice your level of joy or other emotion on the scale of 0 to 10; it should have gone up.
4. If your sense of wellbeing hasn't increased, go to the Trouble-shooting chapter on page 259 to find out what to do next.
5. Think of one thing you're grateful for today and bask in your appreciation of it for a few moments.

Optional Extras for Maximum Benefit

6. Repeat the tapping script as many times as you have time for (and once is better than never!) with the aim of increasing your chosen positive emotion to 10.
7. Do one small, practical and manageable thing today to help you experience more joy.
8. Write down your reflections in your journal or workbook.
9. Share with the Facebook support group:
   * how you feel about your Blissful Day and what came up for you during the tapping
   * what action you're going to take today to create more joy
   * one thing you're grateful for
10. Read a few comments from the other mums and share some encouragement, support or inspiration to help you and your tribe members stay on track.

Day 9: Creating your Blissful Day: Part 2 – tapping script

Side of hand: Even though my image of a Blissful Day is so far from my reality, I acknowledge that this is just the way it is right now.

Even though it seems impossible to experience my Blissful Day right now, I'm open to accepting myself and my life.

Even though I don't know how to bridge the gap between my life right now and my Blissful Day, I choose to know that every day I tap, my Blissful Day is getting closer.

Top of head: I want to have a Blissful Day.

Eyebrow: Part of me doesn't believe it's possible.

Side of eye: Part of me craves that feeling of my Blissful Day.

Under eye: I wonder what it would be like to experience blissful-day energy.

Under nose: I want to experience blissful-day energy now.

Chin: I choose to release all the limiting beliefs that are preventing me from experiencing my Blissful Day.

Collarbone: I'm open to experiencing my blissful-day feeling flowing through every cell of my body.

Under arm: I choose to know that as I tap, the possibility of my Blissful Day is getting closer.

Top of head: I'm open to the possibility of noticing my blissful-day feeling in my body right now.

Eyebrow: I'm noticing where I can feel my blissful-day feeling in my body.

Side of eye:	I'm radiating my blissful-day feeling into every cell of my body.
Under eye:	I'm radiating my blissful-day feeling into every fibre of my being.
Under nose:	I'm radiating my blissful-day feeling all around me.
Chin:	I'm filling my home with my blissful-day energy.
Collarbone:	I'm infusing my children and my parenting with my Blissful Day.
Under arm:	I'm infusing my partner and my relationship [if relevant] with my blissful-day energy.
Top of head:	I'm radiating my blissful-day feeling into my parents and my relationship with them.
Eyebrow:	I'm radiating my blissful-day feeling into my work/housework.
Side of eye:	I'm radiating my blissful-day feeling into the rest of the day.
Under eye:	I'm radiating my blissful-day feeling into the rest of the month.
Under nose:	I'm radiating my blissful-day feeling into the rest of the year.
Chin:	I'm radiating my blissful-day feeling into every aspect of my life.
Collarbone:	I'm radiating my blissful-day feeling into my long, healthy and happy future.
Under arm:	I'm making my blissful-day feeling bigger, brighter and more vivid.
Chest:	[taking a deep breath] Transform.

Day 10

Are you insane?

'The tapping videos have been emotional and empowering for me. I realised that I'm anxious about saying goodbye to my daughter on her first day of school, even though she's been at nursery since she was ten months old! Had some big releases in just five minutes watching the videos! Thank you, Tamara.'
Emily

According to Einstein, the definition of insanity is doing the same thing over and over again and expecting a different result. Well, guess what? If you keep doing what you've been doing it's unlikely that things will change. This challenge gently encourages you to make tiny changes, one at a time. If you follow all the instructions, in a month you'll have created the foundations for permanent and positive change for yourself, your children, your partner, your work, and your health.

We're now a third of the way through of this 30-Day Challenge. Maybe you have resistance coming up. In that case, well done for showing up here anyway. Or maybe you're sailing through, in which case keep up the great work!

How did you get on with the tapping yesterday? I really want you to succeed, so if you didn't get a good result do check out the Troubleshooting chapter on page 259.

I hear many mums saying that things will change *when*... when I have more time; when I get more sleep; when I have more money; when my children are older; when I get a job, etc.

What if that day never comes? Well, obviously your children are going to grow up! But in the meantime, while you're waiting for your life to change you may be living in a state of chaos and overwhelm. And while you're like that, your children are caught up in the energy of your stress and chaos.

I'm not saying this to make you feel guilty: I'm saying it because I really want to help you change NOW. As a fellow mum, I know that anything that makes me calmer makes life better for my daughter, and that in turn makes *me* feel good. I want to help you make your own and your children's lives better right now – not later, not when they grow up, and not if and when there's a blue moon!

Action

1. Rate your level of stress when you think about things not having changed before now from 0 to 10, where 0 is feeling calm, peaceful and light, and 10 is feeling maximum stress. If you can't relate to this issue choose a script from another day that's more relevant to how you're feeling.

2. Follow the tapping script on page 96. Feel free to change my words to describe how you're feeling more accurately.

3. Rate your level of stress again on the same scale as you think about not having things changed before now.

4. If it hasn't gone down, check the Troubleshooting chapter on page 259 to find out what to do next.

5. Think of one thing that you're grateful for today and bask in your appreciation of it for a few moments.

Optional Extras for Maximum Benefit

6. Repeat the tapping script as many times as you have time for (and once is better than never!) with the aim of reducing the intensity to 0.

7. Do one small, practical and manageable thing today that will help you stop repeating the same unhelpful patterns.

8. Write down your reflections in your journal or workbook.

9. Share with the Facebook support group:
   * how you feel about the possibility of changing, and what came up for you during the tapping
   * what action you're going to take today to stop repeating the same unhelpful patterns
   * one thing you're grateful for

10. Read a few comments from the other mums and share some encouragement, support or inspiration to help you and your tribe members stay on track.

11. Glance at your Blissful Day visualisation to keep it fresh and alive in your mind — keep it somewhere easy to see, such as on the wall in the loo, on your phone, in your purse, by your bed, etc.

Day 10: Are you insane? – tapping script

Side of hand: Even though I've been doing the same old things over and over, hoping life would change, I acknowledge that this is where I am right now. Even though I haven't got the time or the energy I need to implement changes, I accept myself and my situation right now. Even though it feels hard to change, I'm open to acknowledging the change I'm making right now by doing this tapping.

Top of head: I've been stuck in a rut.

Eyebrow: I'm repeating the same patterns over and over.

Side of eye: I want my life to improve but I feel stuck.

Under eye: I haven't got enough time or energy to change.

Under nose: Life would be easier if only [eg I had more money/a job/my children were older].

Chin: Change feels hard.

Collarbone: I want to change for good anyway.

Under arm: I'm taking action right now.

Top of head: Even if I can't feel a change yet, I'm tapping anyway.

Eyebrow: I'm open to the possibility of knowing and trusting that change is happening right now.

Side of eye: Rome wasn't built in a day.

Under eye: Change may not happen immediately.

Under nose: I'm creating small changes one tap at a time.

Chin: I'm creating new good habits.

Collarbone: These habits will enable me to create the life I'm looking for.

Under arm: I'm open to the possibility of knowing that I'm creating sustainable change.

Top of head:	I'm open to change bringing me more peace and ease.
Eyebrow:	I'm open to change bringing me more calm and patience.
Side of eye:	I'm open to change bringing me an abundance of energy.
Under eye:	I'm open to change bringing me more joy and laughter.
Under nose:	I'm open to change bringing me more fulfilment.
Chin:	I'm open to change bringing me more magic and fun.
Collarbone:	I'm open to change bringing me a life of miracles.
Under arm:	I'm open to change bringing me a life of abundance.
Chest:	[taking a deep breath] Transform.

Day 11

Can you see the wood for the trees?

'So my forest is one where sometimes I think I know where the path out is, yet something in me chooses not to take it. Maybe the path looks like too much of a challenge... so I'm hoping to continue with the baby steps and hope to add new ones in as I go. That should help me get on the tricky path out of the forest!'
Rosie

Day 11, and you're really going for it. Fantastic!

Today I want to explain why creating positive change in your life has been such a struggle.

Imagine you're lost in a forest. There are lots of paths to choose from, and you can't remember how you got here or which is the way out. Every path you take seems to lead you round in circles. Isn't this how life feels sometimes?

The reason is that when your mind is cluttered with all the things you need to do, haven't done, should have done, should have said, shouldn't have said, etc, it's difficult to think clearly and productively in order to find workable solutions.

You mind needs to be calm to be able to think new thoughts that you can't conceive of right now. When you do EFT it has several effects, including calming your mind, bringing you clarity, and helping you create new thoughts and see solutions.

It's like being lifted up out of a dense forest for an overview that clearly shows the way out. When tapping with my clients I often see their eyes looking to either side as if to access new reaches of their brain as they create new possibilities and new thoughts.

Action

1. Rate your level of belief that you feel lost or can't find a solution from 0 to 10, with 0 not believing this at all and 10 totally believing it. If you can't relate to this issue choose another day's tapping script instead.
2. Follow the tapping script on page 102, changing my words if you need to to describe what you're feeling more accurately.
3. Rate your level of belief that you feel lost or can't find a solution again on the same scale.
4. If it hasn't gone down, check the Troubleshooting chapter on page 259 for what to do next.
5. Think of one thing that you're grateful for today and bask in your appreciation of it for a few moments.

Optional Extras for Maximum Benefit

6. Repeat the tapping script as many times as you have time for (and once is better than never!) with the aim of reducing the intensity to 0.
7. Do one small, practical and manageable thing today to create ease for yourself in your situation right now, remembering that this challenge is helping you to take tiny step after tiny step towards change.
8. Write down your reflections in your journal or workbook.
9. Share with the Facebook support group:
    * in what areas of your life you've been 'lost in the forest'
    * what insights or moments of clarity you've had since starting the challenge
    * what action you're going to take today to create ease for yourself
    * one thing that you're grateful for
10. Read a few comments from the other mums and share some

encouragement, support or inspiration to help you and the members of your tribe to stay on track.

11. Glance at your Blissful Day visualisation to keep it fresh and alive in your mind – keep it somewhere easy to see, such as on the wall in the loo, on your phone, in your purse, by your bed, etc.

Day 11: Can you see the wood for the trees? – tapping script

Side of hand: Even though I'm lost in a forest and I can't find my way, I acknowledge that this is where I am right now.

Even though I keep going down the same path only to end up in the mess I started with, I accept this forest and my lostness.

Even though I've exhausted all solutions to this problem, I'm open to the possibility of trusting that EFT will bring me new clarity and focus.

Top of head: I'm lost in a forest and can't find my way out.

Eyebrow: Maybe it's caused by my overwhelming to-do list.

Side of eye: Maybe it's my exhaustion that's making me feel foggy-headed.

Under eye: Maybe it's that my children are driving me mad.

Under nose: I've tried to think my way out of this problem.

Chin: I'm open to finding a way of letting go of knowing how to find a solution.

Collarbone: I'm open to stilling my mind and becoming present.

Under arm: The more present I become, the more clarity I have.

Top of head: I'm open to the possibility of having new thoughts.

Eyebrow: New thoughts help me get an overview of my life.

Side of eye: Clear new thoughts give me new insights.

Under eye: New insights give me a new perspective on my situation.

Under nose:	I'm open to getting out of my own way so that I can see the bigger picture.
Chin:	I choose to allow new perspectives to enter my mind.
Collarbone:	New perspectives create new solutions.
Under arm:	I choose to attract win-win solutions for myself and my family.
Top of head:	These solutions may come at any time, perhaps while I'm asleep, or daydreaming, or listening to the radio.
Eyebrow:	These solutions will give me clarity about how to make changes in my life.
Side of eye:	I invite new clear and focused thoughts to flow into my life.
Under eye:	I invite new calm and easeful thoughts to flow into my life.
Under nose:	I invite attractive new perspectives to enter my mind.
Chin:	I invite exciting win-win solutions for me and my family to enter my mind.
Collarbone:	I'm allowing new trusting and peaceful thoughts to flow into my life.
Under arm:	I'm allowing new fun and joyful thoughts to flow into my life.
Chest:	[taking a deep breath] Transform.

Day 12

What do elephants believe?

'My biggest realisation in this challenge is that perhaps I'm not that bad after all but just needed to get a few things in perspective, and I feel like I'm making that happen now. The best thing has been that the tapping ensures I take a few minutes to myself each day. This challenge is an opportunity to briefly make time for and put yourself first without it impacting on your ability to be a good parent. I found the tapping really relaxing, it gave me time to myself without impacting on parenting and helped me sleep better.' Martina

Elephants are trained to stay close to their owners when they're young by chaining them to a stake in the ground. When they try to break free, they can't. So they learn that when they have a chain around their leg they're trapped. When they grow up they're stronger than the chains and the stakes and could easily pull themselves free, but

because they've learned that struggling to break free causes them pain, they don't even try!

Our core beliefs are created between birth and the age of seven, when the brain is like a sponge and has very little ability to filter what it absorbs. For example the belief 'I'm not important' might arise if everyone's cooing at your new baby brother or sister and nobody's interested in the beautiful picture you've just drawn. We hold on to such beliefs, often unaware that they're woven into the fabric of our being. We just act on them as if they are the truth.

It's estimated that 95 per cent of our behaviour is subconscious. That means that most of it is pre-programmed. And that programming can stop you in your tracks as you set out to achieve your goals, be they being more patient when your child has a tantrum, getting your children to school on time, or spending time with them rather than allowing them screen time.

When your behaviour is triggered by your limiting beliefs, it can prevent you being the parent you aspire to be. This is beyond your conscious control most of the time. Fortunately, with EFT this programming can be changed, and with today's challenge I introduce tapping to release limiting beliefs. This is a large area that's mainly beyond the realm of this book, but here's a taster.

These are some of the common beliefs that mums find limiting in their parenting:

I need to keep the peace. Some mums I've worked with created this belief when they were children. One reason could be that their parents were always arguing, so they tried to stay out of the way or to make things better between them. This could be a contributing factor in only feeling okay when everyone else is happy (with a side effect of getting burnt out by always worrying about everyone else in the family).

I need to get it right. I'm very familiar with this one, which definitely affected my early parenting! One way this can occur is through pressure from your parents/your teacher/yourself to do well as a child – and then as an adult and a parent, striving to get it right and be the perfect mum.

I need to keep busy. If you grew up in a family with a lot going on and no downtime, you may be conditioned to believe that this is normal and desirable. Add to this the pressure to have it all as a mother, a partner, and a career woman, and we end up burning out. Some mums I know don't know how to stop, and in fact stopping makes them feel uncomfortable so they fill up every gap in their time.

Here's a list of common limiting beliefs: have a quick scan and select the one that jumps out as most true for you. You may have to tweak the wording to make it more relevant to you.

- ❋ I need to keep the peace
- ❋ I need to get it right
- ❋ I need to keep busy
- ❋ I'm not good enough
- ❋ I'm not important
- ❋ I'm so unlucky
- ❋ I don't have time
- ❋ There's never enough money
- ❋ I'm scared of failing
- ❋ I'm too young/too old
- ❋ Change takes time
- ❋ I don't have what it takes to change
- ❋ I don't deserve more
- ❋ I should be able to cope better
- ❋ I'm all alone
- ❋ I'm incapable of dealing with what's on my plate

Action

1. Rate each of the above beliefs on a scale from 0 to 10, where 0 means you don't believe it at all and 10 that you totally believe it. If you're aware of other, stronger limiting beliefs, add them to the list.
2. Follow the tapping script on page 109 for your chosen limiting belief. If you can't relate to my words, change them to reflect your belief more accurately.
3. Rate your level of belief again on the same scale.
4. If it hasn't gone down, check the Troubleshooting chapter on page 259 to find out what to do next.
5. Think of one thing that you're grateful for today and bask in your appreciation of it for a few moments.

Optional Extras for Maximum Benefit

6. Repeat the tapping script as many times as you have time for (and once is better than never!) with the aim of reducing the intensity to 0. You can also repeat this with other limiting beliefs that feel strongly true.
7. Do one small, practical and manageable thing today to create a new positive belief about yourself or your situation
8. Write down your reflections in your journal or workbook.
9. Share with the Facebook support group:
   - ❀ how you think your selected belief affects your parenting
   - ❀ any shifts or realizations you had as a result of the tapping
   - ❀ what action you're going to take today to create a new positive belief
   - ❀ one thing you're grateful for
10. Read a few of the other mums' comments and share some encouragement, support or inspiration to help you and the members of your tribe to stay on track.

11. Glance at your Blissful Day visualisation to keep it fresh and alive in your mind – keep it somewhere easy to see, such as on the wall in the loo, on your phone, in your purse, by your bed, etc.

Day 12: What do elephants believe? – tapping script

Side of hand: Even though I have this belief and it makes me feel [state emotion, or guess if you can't identify] and I can feel it in my [state part of body, or guess if you can't tell], I acknowledge these feelings and sensations.

Even though I have this belief and I've probably had it for a long time, and maybe I know where it comes from and maybe I don't, I accept myself anyway.

Even though I have this belief, I'm open to the possibility to softening and releasing it.

Top of head: This belief is stopping me having the life I want.
Eyebrow: It's stopping me being the mum I want to be.
Side of eye: I'm like an elephant chained to a post that can't get away.
Under eye: My belief is like my chain.
Under nose: It's holding me back from being free to live the life I want.
Chin: I probably created it a long time ago.
Collarbone: This belief is stopping me moving forward in life.
Under arm: I want to be free from this belief now.

Top of head: Maybe I can feel compassion for the younger me that created this belief.
Eyebrow: Maybe part of me is judging the younger me.
Side of eye: I'm open to the possibility of knowing that that younger me did the best she could.

Under eye:	I'm open to the possibility of starting to release that limiting belief.
Under nose:	I wonder what life would be like if I was free of this belief.
Chin:	I wonder what positive belief I can replace it with.
Collarbone:	Releasing this will free me to be the mum I want to be.
Under arm:	I want to be free to be me.
Top of head:	I choose to release this belief so that I can be free to be me.
Eyebrow:	I choose to release this belief so I can be the mum I want to be.
Side of eye:	I choose to release this belief so I can have more confidence in myself.
Under eye:	I choose to release this belief so I can have more belief in myself.
Under nose:	I choose to release this belief so I can forgive myself when I get it wrong.
Chin:	I choose to release this belief so I can feel okay about asking for help when I need it.
Collarbone:	I choose to release this so I can believe I'm good enough.
Under arm:	I choose to release this belief so that I become a better role model for my children.
Chest:	[taking a deep breath] Transform.

Day 13

Creating your Blissful Day revisited

'Wow! What a lovely tap. I started on a six and feel like a nine right now. I really took the sensation of my Blissful Day into my heart and it exploded around my body (I call it a joygasm). I'm feeling so peaceful and looking forward to tomorrow's challenge. Thank you.' Natalie

Today we're going do some more EFT on your Blissful Day visualisation of the first week, to ground that visualisation in all the cells of your body.

If you've been struggling with your Blissful Day, try imagining a day that fills you with pleasure and joy – and no guilt! – when you think about it. If that simply means a day that goes smoothly as you do all your normal things, that's great.

When I have a particularly busy or potentially stressful day ahead I visualise the things I need to get done and then infuse the tricky parts of the day with whatever positive qualities I'll need in that moment, such as flow, ease, relaxation, or even miracles.

Esther, a mum who took the 30-Day Challenge online, was frustrated at falling out of her routine of doing five minutes of tapping first thing. Having found time later in the day while her baby was napping, she tapped and reported great results. Her Blissful Day included a deep sense of calm, and after the tapping she noticed 'huge waves of calm washing over me to the point where I felt so peaceful all though my body'.

Action

1. Think of your Blissful Day and rate your level of joy, excitement, peace or happiness on a scale from 0 to 10. This time 0 represents no joy (or other positive emotion selected) at all, and 10 the most possible. This tapping will increase your positive feelings rather than reduce your negative ones.
2. Follow the tapping script on page 115.
3. When focusing on your Blissful Day again, notice your level of joy (or other emotion) on the same scale. It should have gone up.
4. If it hasn't gone up, check the Troubleshooting chapter on page 259 to find out what to do next.
5. Think of one thing that you're grateful for today and bask in your appreciation of it for a few moments.

Optional Extras for Maximum Benefit

6. Repeat the tapping script as many times as you have time for (and once is better than never!) with the aim of increasing your positive emotion to 10.
7. Do one small, practical and manageable thing today to help you experience more joy.
8. Write down your reflections in your journal or workbook.
9. Share with the Facebook support group:
   * how you feel about your Blissful Day
   * what came up for you during the tapping
   * what action you're going to take today to help you experience more joy
   * one thing you're grateful for
10. Read a few comments from the other mums and share some encouragement, support or inspiration to help you and the members of your tribe to stay on track.

11. Glance at your Blissful Day visualisation to keep it fresh and alive in your mind – keep it somewhere easy to see, such as on the wall in the loo, on your phone, in your purse, by your bed, etc.

Day 13: Creating your Blissful Day revisited – tapping script

Side of hand: Even though I want to bring blissful-day energy into my day every day and it feels like a long journey to get there, I acknowledge the parts of my life that are working well.

Even though part of me is resisting the possibility of being able to experience my Blissful Day right now, I'm open to accepting myself and my life just the way it is.

Even though I'm not really sure how to make my Blissful Day happen, I choose to know that with every day I tap, my Blissful Day is getting closer.

Top of head: I want to experience my Blissful Day.

Eyebrow: Part of me still doesn't believe it's possible.

Side of eye: I'm noticing the parts of my day that are going well.

Under eye: I'm celebrating the moments when life flows smoothly.

Under nose: I'm open to the possibility of bringing more of these qualities into every part of my day.

Chin: I'm open to experiencing ease and joy more often in my day.

Collarbone: I choose to infuse positive moments into my day when my life isn't flowing.

Under arm: I'm open to the possibility of becoming more aligned with my Blissful Day.

Top of head: The more aligned I become, the more my life relaxes and softens.

Eyebrow:	I'm open to the possibility that as I tap on my Blissful Day, my Blissful Day may evolve.
Side of eye:	So I'm accepting this day today, just the way it is and just the way it isn't.
Under eye:	The more I accept my day today just as it is, the more aligned I become with my Blissful Day.
Under nose:	I'm allowing myself to feel and experience blissful energy right here, right now.
Chin:	I'm open to allowing blissful energy to radiate all around me.
Collarbone:	I'm infusing blissful energy into my home.
Under arm:	I'm infusing blissful energy into my children and my parenting.
Top of head	I'm infusing blissful energy into my partner and my relationship [if relevant].
Eyebrow:	I'm infusing blissful energy into my parents and my relationship with them.
Side of eye:	I'm radiating blissful energy into my work/housework.
Under eye:	I'm radiating blissful energy into the rest of my day.
Under nose:	I choose to send blissful energy back through my past.
Chin:	I choose to send blissful energy into my future and my children's future.
Collarbone:	I'm infusing blissful energy into every cell of my body.
Under arm:	I'm infusing my Blissful Day with magic and miracles.
Chest:	[taking a deep breath] Transform.

S-J's story

EFT helped my children get to sleep

When I was running this challenge online I invited all the participants to a virtual campfire celebration. This involved everyone bringing their own hot chocolate, glass of wine, or in my case turmeric latte, and marshmallows, smores or raw chocolate and coming together to share stories, ask questions and do some group tapping.

In an ideal world our gathering would have been an in person meetup around a lovely campfire on a warm summer evening. But mums joined the challenge from all corners of the world so an online virtual gathering with no need for a babysitter was a great second-best.

One of S-J's first experiences of EFT was at my one of my virtual online campfires. She wanted to join us but her girls wouldn't settle down to sleep, so I offered to do some tapping with them. I suggested they tap on their teddies. The girls watched me on S-J's phone tapping on my own teddy and followed along with me. We tapped on 'Even though my teddy is really tired and doesn't want to go to sleep, he's a great teddy and I love him very much' etc. After the little girls had repeated my statements and tapped a couple of rounds I suggested to S-J that she continue by tapping on them while saying calming words until they settled. Five minutes later the girls had settled and S-J joined the campfire.

She went on to take part in the 30-Day Challenge. She says:

'Before I started the challenge I felt very low and hopeless. I suffered from anxiety and felt not good enough as a mum. I wondered if I would be able to support my children the way they needed me to. As the 30-Day Challenge progressed there was a definite shift in energy and a sense of resilience that I could draw upon in the moment, which had some wonderful effects on my ability to cope with difficult situations. I also developed an amazing connectedness with my children and started using EFT with them. Physically I felt much brighter and had more energy. Even my husband said to me 'Gosh – you're looking healthier'! The challenge has also changed my ability to love myself and take better care of myself. It's brought a spark back to my life and I experience joy, which is just incredible.' S-J

Day 14

Catch up and recap

'After tapping with you, I began to change the way I thought and acted towards others, knowing that I was the only person who could effect a change if something was annoying me. It's made a huge difference: people started to react differently, in a positive way.' Catherine

You've worked really hard this week, so a big congratulations for showing up every day and creating positive change for you and your family.

If you're behind, this is a great time to catch up. If you're up to speed, it's a great time to review your week. This week you've created a Blissful Day visualisation and done some tapping on it, with the invitation to spend a few moments every day focusing on your perfect or ideal day. By regularly attending to this you're creating currents heading in the direction of Destination Blissful in the sea on which your "*Mum* ship" is sailing, as described on Day 1.

You then addressed the vicious circle that you've probably experienced of doing the same things over and over again and feeling frustrated that nothing was changing. Next you addressed the feeling of being lost and unable to find your way. Tapping creates clarity and new thoughts, like lifting you above a forest with a clear view of the paths through it that you couldn't see when you were down among the trees.

Lastly, we looked at your limiting beliefs and started tapping to reduce them and their effect on you and your parenting. We're just dipping our toes into what's possible with EFT here, as we're only doing five minutes a day for 30 days. Once you're able to fully release your limiting beliefs, literally your whole life can change around you: your thoughts, your feelings, and how people around you respond to you, as Catherine says at the start of this chapter.

Action

1. If you're up to speed and want to create more momentum and do some more tapping, repeat one of the tapping scripts from previous days, or you can simply have a rest day.
2. If you feel you'd benefit from seeing tapping in action, check out the Frazzled to Fabulous Membership Club. Details are on Frazzledtofabulous.com/Bonus.
3. Then do one thing for yourself today – even the smallest thing is good, for example take one deep breath, have an uninterrupted bath, chat with a friend, go for a walk.

Day 15

Getting it right

'I normally go up to my bedroom for peace and quiet to do the challenge, but for some reason I decided to grab five minutes whilst sat with the girls on the sofa. I tapped on how stressed I feel having to choose between being a perfect housewife and being a perfect mother, and my frustration on days where I have no go, no patience and not much productivity. It didn't take very long at all and I felt so full of joy that I wanted to cry. My two-year-old was tapping with me, my stresses shrank ... I thought it impossible to feel like my life is anything but perfect just the way it is. Full of gratitude for my precious girls and all the lovely moments life creates. 😊 😊 🤍*'* Bronte

Halfway! Go you! I'm doing a happy dance for you! What are you going to do to celebrate?

You're making powerful changes. By showing up every day and taking these small actions you're rewiring your brain and creating a new habit. Keep up the great work!

I hope you're sitting comfortably, as I have a story for you today.

A mum who lived in a village far from the nearest well walked every day to fetch water, carrying two large pots that hung on the ends of a pole that she carried across her shoulders. One pot was in perfect condition, whereas the other had a crack in it. Every day when she returned to the village the perfect pot was full but the cracked pot was only half full. The cracked pot was ashamed of her imperfection and her inability to fulfil her task properly. After several months of the mum repeating this journey, the side of the path on which she carried the cracked pot was a mass of wild flowers that had grown as a result of water dripping through the crack.

The cracks and flaws in each of us make us unique and perfect in our imperfection.

Motherhood has the tendency to bring out the worst aspects of perfectionism because we love our children so much and want to give them the best start in life. Some of us try to make life perfect for them and end up getting stressed, overwhelmed and far from able to give our children the 'perfect' life we want for them, which makes us feel even worse!

If you can't relate to this, think of the times you tell yourself 'I should/shouldn't/must/mustn't…' and then when you can't or don't act the way you feel you should, you give yourself a hard time!

I struggled with this for a time. I remember one incident when I was sitting with my daughter and my friend and her daughter in a ball pool, talking about motherhood. I told my friend I would never let my daughter down. My friend wisely replied that she was aiming to be a 'good enough' mother, and that there would be times when she would let her daughter down. Luckily I learnt to accept my imperfections and have compassion for myself as well as for my daughter when I let her down.

So consider the areas where you're trying hard to get it right and make it perfect for your children.

Action

1. Rate your need to get it right from 0 to 10, where at 0 you don't feel that need at all and at 10 you feel you need to get it absolutely right. If you can't relate to this issue choose a script from another day that's more relevant to how you're feeling.
2. Follow the tapping script on page 127. Feel free to change my words to describe how you're feeling more accurately.
3. After tapping, rate your level of needing to get it right again on the same scale.
4. If it hasn't gone down, check the Troubleshooting chapter on page 259 to find out what to do next.
5. Think of one thing that you're grateful for today and bask in your appreciation of it for a few moments.

Optional Extras for Maximum Benefit

6. Repeat the tapping script as many times as you have time for (and once is better than never!) with the aim of reducing the intensity to 0.
7. Do one small, practical and manageable thing today that will help you parent from a place of being good enough rather than one of needing to get it right.
8. Write down your reflections in your journal or workbook.
9. Share with the Facebook support group:
    * your need to get things right or be a perfect mum, and what came up for you during the tapping
    * what action you're going to take today to parent from a place of being good enough rather than trying to get it right
    * one thing you're grateful for
10. Read a few comments from other mums in the Facebook support group and share some encouragement, support or inspiration to help you and the members of your tribe to stay

on track.

11. Glance at your Blissful Day visualisation to keep it fresh and alive in your mind – keep it somewhere easy to see, such as on the wall in the loo, on your phone, in your purse, by your bed, etc.

Day 15: Getting it right – tapping script

Side of hand: Even though I need to get it right, I acknowledge this need and the pressure I put on myself.

Even though I really want to get it right for myself and for my children, I'm open to accepting myself just the way I am, and my life just the way it is.

Even though I really want to get it right, I choose to know that I'm a good-enough mum.

Top of head: I need to get it right.
Eyebrow: I'm really hard on myself.
Side of eye: I beat myself up when I think I've got it wrong.
Under eye: This pressure I put on myself.
Under nose: I try to be a better mum.
Chin: I try to be the mum I didn't have [OR] I try to reach my mum's high standards.

Collarbone: The standards I set myself are hard to reach.
Under arm: So I end up setting myself up to fail.

Top of head: Maybe I can have some compassion for myself.
Eyebrow: Maybe I can recognise the things that are going well.
Side of eye: Maybe I can learn to be kinder to myself.
Under eye: Maybe I can learn to accept that I will make mistakes.
Under nose: I'm remembering that I'm human.
Chin: Humans make mistakes.
Collarbone: My children love me whether I make mistakes or not.
Under arm: My children learn from seeing me making mistakes and acknowledging them.

Top of head:	I'm open to the possibility of bringing more acceptance into my life and my parenting.
Eyebrow:	I'm open to the possibility of bringing more ease into my life and my parenting.
Side of eye:	I'm open to the possibility of bringing more trust into my life and my parenting.
Under eye:	I'm open to the possibility of bringing more forgiveness into my life and my parenting.
Under nose:	I'm open to the possibility of bringing more peace into my life and my parenting.
Chin:	I'm open to the possibility of bringing more calm into my life and my parenting.
Collarbone:	I'm open to the possibility of bringing more joy into my life and my parenting.
Under arm:	I'm open to the possibility of bringing more love into my life and my parenting.
Chest:	[taking a deep breath] Transform.

Day 16

Are you being pulled in too many directions?

'I could really relate to all the feelings of overwhelm in this challenge, often feel like I'm on the hamster wheel juggling all the balls. After tapping tonight, I'm feeling very uplifted. I've decided to make a change by slowing down and learning to say no. Life can be hectic, and I'd like to focus on making a calm environment for my family, live in the moment and enjoy doing less rather than rushing from one thing to the next. Today I'm grateful for EFT and the new tools I'm learning. I played a 'tapping game' to help my son settle himself to sleep tonight (something I've been struggling with): I tapped his fingers whilst singing Tommy Thumb and it worked, on the third time I sang it he was fast asleep 👍*'* Gemma

You're on the home stretch now! Keep going, and start noticing the changes. At this point in my online challenge mums were mentioning how much lighter and more joyful they were feeling, and I hope you are too.

Maybe you'll have noticed that you're feeling more peaceful, sleeping better or have more patience around your children. If you have, big congratulations are coming your way. If you haven't, don't worry – everyone changes at a different rate. You're doing a great job! Either way, don't let your great work be for nothing. KEEP GOING!

One of the biggest reasons stopping mums having a better, easier and calmer life for themselves and their families is that they get overwhelmed by everything they have to do.

Mums tell me they're juggling too many balls, on a never-ending hamster wheel, being pulled in too many directions at once. Since you've bought this book I'm sure you can relate to this – and I've definitely been there!

It might be the school run, mealtimes and bedtimes mixed in with work, managing a home, and for some also being a carer, coping with illness and lots more.

It's not unusual for mums to feel overwhelmed, and not surprisingly this scored very high with mums who did the online challenge and completed the survey. One of these was Mary, who shared that she

had received the overwhelm tapping video at the perfect time as she'd reached 10 on the scale. After following the tapping routine the intensity fell to just 4. She also realized that a lot of her overwhelm was coming from pressure she was putting on herself.

Action

1. Rate your level of overwhelm from 0 to 10, where 0 is not at all overwhelmed and 10 is totally overwhelmed. If you can't relate to this issue choose a script from another day that's more relevant to how you're feeling.
2. Follow the tapping script on the next page. Feel free to change my words to describe how you're feeling more accurately.
3. Rate your level of overwhelm again on the same scale
4. If it hasn't gone down, check the Troubleshooting chapter on page 259 to find out what to do next
5. Think of one thing that you're grateful for today and bask in your appreciation of it for a few moments.

Optional Extras for Maximum Benefit

6. Repeat the tapping script as many times as you have time for (and once is better than never!) with the aim of reducing the intensity to 0.
7. Do one small, practical and manageable thing today to reduce your level of overwhelm.
8. Write down your reflections in your journal or workbook.
9. Share with the Facebook support group:
   * what makes you feel overwhelmed
   * what came up for you during the tapping
   * what action you're going to take today to change this
   * one thing you're grateful for
10. Read a few of the other mums' comments and share some encouragement, support or inspiration to help you and the members of your tribe stay on track.
11. Glance at your Blissful Day visualisation to keep it fresh and alive in your mind – keep it somewhere easy to see, such as on the wall in the loo, on your phone, in your purse, by your bed, etc.

Day 16: Are you being pulled in too many directions? – tapping script

Side of hand: Even though I'm feeling overwhelmed and I can feel it in my [state part of body, or guess if you can't identify it] and it feels like [state body sensation, or guess if you can't identify it], I acknowledge those feelings and sensations.
Even though I'm so overwhelmed, I accept myself in this situation.
Even though there's so much to do, I'm open to the possibility that there's an easier way.

Top of head: I'm noticing this overwhelm and where I feel it in my body.

Eyebrow: I acknowledge this uncomfortable sensation of overwhelm and where I feel it in my body.

Side of eye: I'm overwhelmed by the thought of everything I need to do.

Under eye: I'm being pulled in so many directions at once.

Under nose: I'm juggling so many balls and I feel like I'm on a never-ending hamster wheel.

Chin: All the things that I'm overwhelmed about keep me awake at night.

Collarbone: Overwhelm prevents me being present with my children.

Under arm: It even stops me being present with myself.

Top of head: I'm open to the possibility of releasing some of this overwhelm.

Eyebrow: I'm taking a deep breath now. [Take a deep breath]

Side of eye: I'm noticing my body right now.

Under eye:	I'm acknowledging how my body feels in this moment.
Under nose:	I'm open to the possibility of accepting myself and this overwhelm.
Chin:	Accepting myself just as I am, and just as I'm not.
Collarbone:	I wonder what life would be like if I wasn't overwhelmed.
Under arm:	I wonder what I'd be feeling if I released this overwhelm.
Top of head:	I wonder if there's a way of not feeling overwhelmed despite having so much to do.
Eyebrow:	Maybe I can release some of this overwhelm.
Side of eye:	I'm noticing my feet on the ground.
Under eye:	I'm noticing my breath just as it is right now.
Under nose:	I'm open to the possibility of feeling calm despite my to-do list.
Chin:	I'm open to the possibility of feeling peace despite my to-do list.
Collarbone:	I'm open to the possibility of infusing trust into my situation.
Under arm:	I choose to accept myself and my situation just the way they are.
Chest:	[taking a deep breath] Transform.

Day 17

What do you deserve?

'This is something I struggle with, as I've always felt like I don't deserve. I feel like unless I work really hard at something, I don't deserve the results. This makes it hard for me to take time for myself and know that my needs are important. The tapping session was really powerful, and this challenge is absolutely helping me to be more accepting and to relax more rather than punish myself with my thoughts. I feel calmer as usual after the tapping.' Andy

Just two weeks to go! Can you believe you've stuck with this so far? I'm so happy for you! And remember, the key to success is making this a daily habit.

Do you allow yourself to receive help, support, love, etc?

Do you feel you deserve to have the good things in life? Do you feel you deserve your Blissful Day?

Are you allowing yourself to receive the wonderful changes that have been happening to you since starting the challenge, or is part of you resisting or feeling not good enough, not deserving because

❁ you aren't a good-enough mother? (I definitely used to feel that!)
❁ you're used to struggling: it's what your family does (and this has been another of my own challenges)

❀ you can't have a better life than those around you
❀ life as a mum should be hard?

What were you taught as a child about deserving the good things in life? Did you have to toe the line? Earn respect or approval? Something else?

Notice what feelings and thoughts arise as you read this, and if you relate to any of these beliefs consider doing Day 12's 'What Do Elephants Believe' tapping exercise on them.

'Since the birth of Susan's first child she had put a lot of pressure on herself to be the best mum she could. This resulted in her needs ending up at the bottom of the pile in terms of priorities. Towards the end of the challenge she reflected that as she approached the end of the day she was craving a soak

in a hot bath. At that point she could easily have got stuck into tidying the kitchen and clearing away the toys, but instead she thought 'I've spent the whole day wiping noses, making food, clearing and tidying up the continuous mess. I'm doing such a great job! I so deserve my bath. I AM important, and in order to keep up the great work I need to take care of myself!'

By increasing your sense of deservingness you show your children that it's okay and necessary to prioritise your own needs and treat yourself and allow yourself to receive compliments and gifts rather than deflecting them or pushing them away.

Action

1. Rate how deserving you feel on a scale of 0 to 10, where at 0 you don't feel at all deserving and at 10 you feel completely deserving. If you can't relate to this issue choose a script from another day that's more relevant to how you're feeling.
2. Follow the tapping script on the next page. Feel free to change my words to describe how you're feeling more accurately.
3. Rate your level of deservingness again from 0 to 10 on the same scale.
4. If it hasn't gone up, check the Troubleshooting chapter on page 259 to find out what to do next.
5. Think of one thing you're grateful for today and bask in your appreciation of it for a few moments.

Optional Extras for Maximum Benefit

6. Repeat the tapping script as many times as you have time for (and once is better than never!) with the aim of reducing the intensity to 0.
7. Do one small, practical and manageable thing today that you would do if you truly knew you were deserving.
8. Write down your reflections in your journal or workbook.
9. Share with the Facebook support group:
   * your relationship with feeling deserving
   * what came up in the tapping
   * what action you're going to take today to increase your feeling of deservingness
   * one thing you're grateful for
10. Read a few of the other mums' comments and share some encouragement, support or inspiration to help you and the members of your tribe stay on track.

11. Glance at your Blissful Day visualisation to keep it fresh and alive in your mind — keep it somewhere easy to see, such as on the wall in the loo, on your phone, in your purse, by your bed, etc.

Day 17: What do you deserve? – tapping script

Side of hand: Even though my needs get pushed to the bottom of the pile, I acknowledge that this is my situation right now.

Even though I'm not very good at creating time for myself and my needs, I accept myself and my situation.

Even though I feel I have to put everybody else first, I choose to know that I'm important, worthy and deserving.

Top of head: I always push my needs to the bottom of the pile.
Eyebrow: I'm not good at creating time for myself.
Side of eye: I feel I have to put everybody else first.
Under eye: It's hard to look after my own needs.
Under nose: Taking time for myself makes me feel guilty.
Chin: I feel as if I don't deserve it.
Collarbone: It's hard to ask for help.
Under arm: Other mums seem to cope better than me.

Top of head: If I don't take care of myself I get more stressed.
Eyebrow: When I get more stressed my family suffers.
Side of eye: Part of me feels I should be able to do it all.
Under eye: Part of me feels guilty when I don't cope well.
Under nose: Part of me doesn't feel that I deserve help.
Chin: Maybe I can have some compassion for myself just the way I am.
Collarbone: Maybe I can stop comparing myself to others.
Under arm: Each mother has her own journey and struggles.

Top of head: I choose to let go of my judgements about what I can and can't cope with.

Eyebrow:	I choose to let go of my 'shoulds' about my mothering.
Side of eye:	I choose to allow myself to pay attention to my own needs.
Under eye:	I choose to know that I deserve to get my needs met too.
Under nose:	I choose to know that when I let go of wanting to know how to resolve this situation, new possibilities will arise.
Chin:	I'm open to win-win solutions showing themselves to me, even if I can't see them right now.
Collarbone:	I'm open to finding a way of getting my needs met so that I can be an even better mother.
Under arm:	I'm open to magic and miracles coming my way!
Chest:	[taking a deep breath] Transform.

Day 18

What are you putting off?

'Can you believe that when I filled in the questionnaire at the start of the challenge, procrastination was the only one to score 10! So today's tapping was fab for me... I get very irritated and angry with myself for procrastinating. My reaction is to get overwhelmed and mentally freeze, and then I seem to be incapable of taking any practical steps to move forward. It drives my partner mad. Only when things get to a state of crisis do I start firefighting! Anyway, since tapping today I put my phone down and got some forms filled in!' Molly

I'm so happy to see you here again today!

Do you have so much to do that you sometimes feel paralysed and don't know where to start?

Do you fritter away your time, immersing yourself in social media so you don't hear your child trying to have a conversation with you?

Do you put things off until the last minute and then get so stressed you don't know what to do first?

Do you do all the little things in order to avoid doing what really needs to be done?

Procrastination is something I'm definitely guilty of. In fact while writing this book I've noticed myself flicking over to Facebook rather than staying focused on the task in hand!

When there's too much to do it can give rise to feeling stressed and overwhelmed, which in turn prevents us thinking clearly and focusing.

I used to hate working on my allotment, but I love the end results – yummy, fresh, home-grown organic veg. It got so overgrown that when I tried to think where I should start I was overwhelmed. So one year I decided to take a different approach – to go there on as many days in the week as I had time for (usually three or four) and spend 30 minutes doing anything that felt easy and manageable, without putting pressure on myself to achieve anything at all. The results were amazing: we had the biggest crops ever that year. Now I just need to apply those principles to my home, which is harder because it's not as easy to be unattached to the outcome.

The more attached to the outcome we are, the harder it can be. This tapping routine will help you release stress and overwhelm so that you can see the next tiny, manageable step to take more clearly.

Action

1. Think about a task you've been putting off. Rate how your procrastination feels from 0 to 10, where at 0 it doesn't affect you at all and at 10 you're totally consumed by it. If you can't relate to this issue choose a script from another day that's more relevant to how you're feeling.

2. Follow the tapping script on the next page. Feel free to change my words to describe how you're feeling more accurately.

3. Thinking about doing that task now, rate your feeling of procrastination again on the same scale.

4. If it hasn't gone down, check the Troubleshooting chapter on page 259 to find out what to do next.

5. Think of one thing that you're grateful for today and bask in your appreciation of it for a few moments.

Optional Extras for Maximum Benefit

6. Repeat the tapping script as many times as you have time for (and once is better than never!) with the aim of reducing the intensity to 0.

7. Take one small, manageable and practical step towards completing the task you've been putting off. Just for fun, you could put your timer on and see if you can get a small task done in 10 minutes or less. For example, if you need to declutter you could start with one small drawer, or if your bathroom needs repainting you could gather the materials together in a crate so that when you have a larger chunk of time you'll be ready to get going.

8. Write down your reflections in your journal or workbook.

9. Share with the Facebook support group:
   ❋ how procrastination affects you, your parenting or your children

❋ what came up in the tapping

❋ what action you're going to take today that you've been putting off

❋ one thing you're grateful for

10. Read a few comments from other mums in the Facebook support group and share some encouragement, support or inspiration to help you and the members of your tribe to stay on track.

11. Glance at your Blissful Day visualisation to keep it fresh and alive in your mind – keep it somewhere easy to see, such as on the wall in the loo, on your phone, in your purse, by your bed, etc.

Day 18: What are you putting off? – tapping script

Side of hand: Even though I'm avoiding doing important things, I acknowledge my habit and my situation. Even though I feel stressed about doing those things and stressed about not doing them, I still accept myself.
Even though I'm too stressed to figure a way out of this situation, I'm open to the possibility of releasing some of this stress now.

Top of head: Maybe I'm trying so hard to get it right that I end up getting nothing done.

Eyebrow: Maybe I'm worried about getting on with stuff because I'll be judged on the results.

Side of eye: Even when I do take action there's always more to do.

Under eye: Maybe I'm filled with dread at the thought of getting on with it all.

Under nose: Maybe I'm feeling too overwhelmed to know where to start.

Chin: Maybe I get sucked into the black hole of social media.

Collarbone: Maybe I only function under pressure, so I always wait till the last minute to do things.

Under arm: There's too much to do – the school run, packed lunches, laundry, dishes [add from your to-do list!]

Top of head: I'm acknowledging all my procrastinating habits now.

Eyebrow:	I'm acknowledging that procrastinating makes me feel stressed, overwhelmed, frustrated, etc.
Side of eye:	Maybe I can allow these feelings to be present.
Under eye:	By acknowledging these feelings, I can start releasing them.
Under nose:	I can start allowing clarity and calm to replace these feelings.
Chin:	Clarity and calm help me take action.
Collarbone:	I choose to have compassion for the part of me that procrastinates.
Under arm:	Maybe this procrastinating behaviour has been there for a long time.
Top of head:	I'm open to finding a new healthy relationship with things that need doing.
Eyebrow:	I choose to find a way of doing this, even if I don't know how.
Side of eye:	I choose to be curious about this new way of being.
Under eye:	I choose to trust that tapping is opening up new ways of thinking and being.
Under nose:	I'm open to being surprised at how easy it is to create new ways of getting things done.
Chin:	I'm inviting efficiency and productivity into my life.
Collarbone:	I'm open to the possibility of getting things done easily and effortlessly.
Under arm:	I choose to have a great day, no matter what I do or don't get done today!
Chest:	[taking a deep breath] Transform.

Day 19

How many thoughts are bouncing around in your mind right now?

'I'm definitely guilty of overthinking and have felt exhausted just from overthinking in the past. I've noticed how my thoughts have calmed over the course of the past two weeks or so, so something is working. In fact I felt my overthinking was at a two at the beginning of this tapping exercise – quite a surprise.' Rosie

Do you ever wake up in the morning feeling there's so much to do that you don't know where to start, and just thinking about it gives you a headache? Believe me, I've been there, and even now, trying to complete the writing of this book regularly sends me into a tailspin! Most of the time I can nip those feelings in the bud with some EFT, but twice in the last year my book-creation stress levels rose too high and before I knew it I was ill – once with flu that took me four weeks to recover from, and once for just a few days, as I was able to notice the pattern and tap it out.

Many mums tell me they have so many thoughts spinning around in their head so much of the time that they find it hard to focus, to prioritise, to be present with their children, or to sleep; sometimes their thoughts keep them awake at night, often worrying about things that happened yesterday, things that are coming up tomorrow, things that should or shouldn't have been said, etc.

Overthinking can be so all-consuming that there's no room left for finding clarity or focus, or for prioritising. And as a consequence, the little people in our lives suffer with mums who find it hard to be present with them.

If you manage to catch yourself overthinking, take a moment to apply the SOS process introduced on Day 2 on page 48.

Action

1. Rate your level of overthinking or how cluttered your mind feels on a scale from 0 to 10, where 0 is calm, peace and light and 10 is the highest intensity you can imagine. If you can't relate to this issue choose a script from another day that's more relevant to how you're feeling.

2. Follow the tapping script on the next page. Feel free to change my words to describe how you're feeling more accurately.

3. Rate your level of overthinking or how cluttered your mind feels again on the same scale.

4. If it hasn't gone down, check the Troubleshooting chapter on page 259 to find out what to do next.

5. Think of one thing that you're grateful for today and bask in your appreciation of it for a few moments.

Optional Extras for Maximum Benefit

6. Repeat the tapping script as many times as you have time for (and once is better than never!) with the aim of reducing the intensity to 0.

7. Do one small, practical and manageable thing today to release some of that overthinking and create calm in your mind.

8. Write down your reflections in your journal or workbook.

9. Share with the Facebook support group:
    * how overthinking and a cluttered mind affect you
    * what came up for you during the tapping
    * what action you're going to take today to release some of that overthinking
    * one thing you're grateful for

10. Read a few comments from the other mums and share some encouragement, support or inspiration to help you and the members of your tribe to stay on track.

11. Glance at your Blissful Day visualisation to keep it fresh and alive in your mind – keep it somewhere easy to see, such as on the wall in the loo, on your phone, in your purse, by your bed, etc.

Day 19: How many thoughts are bouncing around in your mind right now? – tapping script

Side of hand: Even though I can't stop the thoughts spinning round in my head, I acknowledge this feeling and allow it to be here.

Even though my thoughts stop me sleeping, having clarity and being present with my children, I accept myself just as I am.

Even though these thoughts give me a headache and stop me thinking clearly and knowing what needs to be done, I'm open to the possibility of calming my mind and my thoughts.

Top of head: All these thoughts in my head keep me stressed.

Eyebrow: My thoughts are exhausting.

Side of eye: They stop me sleeping and having focus and clarity.

Under eye: My thoughts are stopping me being present with my children.

Under nose: They stop me doing what needs to be done.

Chin: They give me headaches.

Collarbone: I have so many thoughts, worries, fears, anxieties, what ifs, etc.

Under arm: My mind keeps looping through everything that happened today.

Top of head: I can't stop thinking about all the things I did and the things I shouldn't have done.

Eyebrow: I can't stop thinking about all the things I didn't do and the things I should have done.

Side of eye: There's so much to do tomorrow, next week, next month…

Under eye:	How am I going to fit it all in?
Under nose:	It's completely exhausting.
Chin:	I wonder what it would be like to have a calm, still mind.
Collarbone:	I'm starting to release all these thoughts and calming my mind now.
Under arm:	I want to have clarity and release my distorted thoughts.
Top of head:	I'm taking a full, deep breath now. [Take a deep breath]
Eyebrow:	I'm infusing more ease and calm into my mind.
Side of eye:	I'm infusing more focus and confidence into my mind.
Under eye:	I'm infusing more clarity and peace into my mind.
Under nose:	I'm infusing more relaxation and joy into my mind.
Chin:	I'm infusing more acceptance and trust into my mind.
Collarbone:	I'm infusing more love and connection into my mind.
Under arm:	I'm infusing more magic and miracles into my mind.
Chest:	[taking a deep breath] Transform.

Day 20

Creating your Blissful Day revisited

'After doing the tapping this morning I feel great. The things I would love to change are getting angry at times due to having no time, and rushing with the kids. But saying this, after these weeks of tapping I have felt so much calmer, and the morning school runs have gone so much better.' Charlotte

So here we are again with your Blissful Day.

Has your Blissful Day evolved since you started?

Is it easier to imagine or visualise?

Is it a reality right now?

When Alice reflected on her weekend away with her partner, she felt it couldn't have been more perfect, but she was also aware of an uneasy feeling as their children hadn't been with them, which she related to 'the mother's eternal guilt'. The children were content away from their parents. She said she would have loved to be able to let go and relax a bit more, but she was on edge. I wonder if she could have increased her relaxation and enjoyment if she'd tapped to release that uneasy feeling of guilt and being on edge?

For years I've been visualising a beautiful garden room at the back of our house. It's felt utterly impossible to make it a reality, but I still continue to dream about how I'll feel when I have my big garden room. I imagine the long table at one end and the relaxation area with comfy chairs at the other. We love running our EFT workshops from home and we invite the participants to bring food to share for lunch sitting round our kitchen table, but if there are more than ten people it can get a bit too cosy for comfort! My dream is to be able to seat 20 people comfortably. To keep my dream alive, I've created a vision board with images and words about how I want the garden room to look and feel. It's hanging on the kitchen cupboard, and every time I look at it I feel happy dreaming about it.

Dream big! Allow your imagination to run wild and be playful with your ideas today.

Action

1. Think of your Blissful Day and rate your level of joy, excitement, peace, happiness etc on a scale from 0 to 10. This time 0 represents no positive emotion at all and 10, the most possible; this tapping will increase your positive feelings rather than reducing your negative ones.

2. Follow the tapping script on the next page. Feel free to change my words to describe how you're feeling more accurately.

3. When focusing on your Blissful Day again, notice your level of joy or other positive emotion on the 0-10 scale – it should have gone up.

4. If it hasn't gone up check the Troubleshooting chapter on page 259 to find out what to do next.

5. Think of one thing you're grateful for today and bask in your appreciation of it for a few moments.

Optional Extras for Maximum Benefit

6. Repeat the tapping script as many times as you have time for (and once is better than never!) with the aim of increasing your joy to 10.

7. Do one small, practical and manageable thing today to help you experience more joy.

8. Write down your reflections in your journal or workbook.

9. Share with the Facebook support group:
   - how you feel about your Blissful Day
   - what came up for you during the tapping
   - what action you're going to take today to create more joy for yourself
   - one thing you're grateful for

10. Read a few comments from the other mums and share some encouragement, support or inspiration to help you and the members of your tribe stay on track.

11. Glance at your Blissful Day visualisation to keep it fresh and alive in your mind – keep it somewhere easy to see, such as on the wall in the loo, on your phone, in your purse, by your bed, etc.

Day 20: Creating your Blissful Day revisited – tapping script

Side of hand: Even though I want to bring even more of my Blissful Day energy into my daily life, I choose to appreciate the changes I've already experienced. Even though a small part of me is still resisting the possibility of being able to fully experience my Blissful Day right, I'm open to the possibility of releasing that resistance now.

Even though I'm beginning to experience some blissful moments, I'm open to the possibility of experiencing even more of them, whether my life has changed or not.

Top of head: My Blissful Day is getting closer and closer.

Eyebrow: I don't think I can make any more changes at the moment.

Side of eye: Part of me can't allow more blissful feelings because of [state reasons eg, children, illness, money problems, lack of support etc].

Under eye: Maybe part of me feels I don't deserve a Blissful Day.

Under nose: These obstacles are stopping me experiencing more blissful energy.

Chin: I'm open to recognising the things I can change and the things that I can't.

Collarbone: I'm open to accepting the things I can't change.

Under arm: I'm open to knowing and trusting that it's possible to have blissful energy anyway.

Top of head: I'm open to the possibility of infusing blissful energy into my life.

Eyebrow:	I'm infusing blissful energy into every cell of my body.
Side of eye:	I'm noticing where in my body I can feel blissful energy [guess if you don't know].
Under eye:	I'm allowing this feeling and sensation to infuse into the rest of me.
Under nose:	I'm allowing this feeling and sensation to infuse into my day today.
Chin:	I'm allowing this feeling and sensation to radiate around me.
Collarbone:	I'm infusing this feeling and sensation into my home.
Under arm:	I'm infusing this feeling and sensation into my children and my parenting.
Top of head:	[if relevant] I'm infusing this feeling and sensation into my partner and my relationship.
Eyebrow:	I'm infusing this feeling and sensation into my parents and my relationship with them.
Side of eye:	I'm infusing this feeling and sensation into my work/my housework.
Under eye:	I'm infusing this feeling and sensation into the rest of my day.
Under nose:	I'm infusing this feeling and sensation back through my past.
Chin:	I'm infusing this feeling and sensation into my future and my children's futures.
Collarbone:	I'm infusing this feeling and sensation into every cell of my body.
Under arm:	I'm infusing my Blissful Day with magic and miracles.
Chest:	[Taking a deep breath] Transform.

Elizabeth Mary's story

Birth trauma gone in 20 minutes

I first discovered Tamara and Peter and EFT when I attended a Birth Trauma Workshop some eight years ago.

To be honest, if I hadn't been heavily pregnant I might have run out of the room when I arrived – late – and saw a room full of people doing this weird 'tapping' thing! Thank goodness I stayed; that day changed my life forever.

Not only did I get cured of the trauma of my first birth and the fear of my second, I was able to cancel my elected C-section and experience the most wonderfully empowering delivery of my second baby naturally and safely with no drugs or intervention – and he weighed 10lbs 3ozs!

Struggling with two children under two, I returned to Tamara and Peter's trusted expertise to learn how to use EFT on myself to calm my nerves, frustration and paranoia around not being a good-enough mum. Enlightened and excited about the power of EFT tapping, I then trained with them to become a qualified Level 2 Practitioner. Fast forward another six years and I've moved from pure EFT practitioner to running a thriving coaching business that incorporates EFT.

I literally thank God for EFT tapping, and Tamara and Peter for introducing me to it and supporting me ever since.

Elizabeth Mary's 9-year-old daughter Izzy's story: Tappy Bear helps children tap

I learnt tapping from my mum. She used to use it on me when I had nightmares and we use it when I'm worried or upset about something. It's helped me with arguments and difficult situations with friends.

We have a Tappy Bear in our house and Mum sometimes lends him to other children when they need some help. Tappy is a special bear with buttons on the tapping points and when he goes to other people's houses they find it easier to tap. They often decide on one of their own bears to become their Tappy Bear too.

Day 21

Catch up and recap

'I got so much out of the tapping and have managed to keep a wonderful level of calmness. I have learnt so much about dealing with the stresses and strains of daily life! The tapping helped me see where I was trying too hard to achieve things, and how in letting go and not trying to control outcomes I was much more relaxed and could get caught up in the moment.' Debby

It's Day 21, and we're on the home stretch! You're awesome! This is the final third of our tapping together.

If you're behind, this is your catch-up day. If you're up to speed, it's a great time to review your week. This week you've starting releasing perfectionism, overwhelm, procrastination and overthinking, and increasing your sense of deservingness – all common issues for frazzled mums.

If you've been tapping every day you'll have created a rhythm for yourself and will be feeling calmer and more relaxed, perhaps benefiting from some unexpected positive side effects of daily chipping away at the edges of what's holding you back from a happier life. Some mums who did the online challenge shared with me that physical symptoms such as period pains eased or disappeared, and people around them noticed that they were happier.

Everyone changes and evolves at a different pace. If you haven't experienced this kind of improvement and want some tips on getting better results, check out the Troubleshooting chapter on page 259 for some ideas.

Action

1. If you're up to speed and want to create more momentum and do some more tapping, then either repeat one of the tapping scripts from previous days or simply have a rest day.

2. If you feel you'd benefit from seeing tapping in action, check out the Frazzled to Fabulous Membership Club. Details are on Frazzledtofabulous.com/Bonus.

3. Do one thing for yourself today. Even the smallest thing is good: for example smell a flower in the garden, listen to your favourite song, go for a jog. I recommend spending five minutes dancing round your kitchen to your favourite music! Family members can join in.

Day 22

Anxiety

'That was amazing. At the start of the tapping I had a lot of anxiety form in my stomach, but as I went through it and concentrated on it, it soon went away to be replaced with a lovely calm feeling.' Sandy

It's Day 22! Can you believe it? You're nearly there!

How is it going?

Are you noticing changes in your life? In your stress levels, with your children, your productivity, your joy? Think back to how you were a few weeks ago…

Has anyone commented on changes they've noticed in you?

What has your biggest realisation or 'aha' moment been so far?

When tapping on anxiety it's possible to get good results simply by tapping on the word 'anxiety', but it works even better if you're able to pinpoint the specific things that make you anxious. I invite you to make a list of the things that make you anxious. For instance

* I've got an appraisal coming up at work
* I've been asked to a meeting at school to discuss my child's behaviour
* My child is such a fussy eater and I worry about his health
* I snapped at my mum when she came over to help with the children

Sometimes you can feel anxious without knowing why. If that's the case, you can tap on the physical sensations of the anxiety instead.

Cheryl shared that she suffers from anxiety when she has too much to do. She works from home and home-educates her daughter. On the day she was doing the anxiety tapping she had a particularly anxiety-provoking day. Her daughter bounded into her bedroom an hour earlier than usual, ready for the day, leaving her little time to prepare the presentation she was due to give while her daughter was at swimming club. On top of that the Wi-Fi stopped working and she spent ages waiting on the phone for the engineers to answer. Trying to juggle an attention-seeking daughter, explain to the

engineer that rebooting the system for the hundredth time was not going to make any difference, and rush the washing in from the garden as it had started to rain was usually a recipe for major anxiety, overwhelm and stress. On this particular day the tapping in the morning had increased her sense of resilience, and although it was a really tough day that left her exhausted, she remained calm and didn't lose her cool!

Thinking of your biggest anxiety and try to identify the cause – if you can't, work on the physical sensations that go with the anxiety.

Action

1. Rate your biggest anxiety and where you feel it in your body on a scale of 0 to 10, with 0 not anxious at all and 10 the most anxious you can imagine. If you know the reason for your anxiety, tune into your feelings about it; otherwise tune into your general level of anxiety. If you can't relate to this issue choose a script from another day that's more relevant to how you're feeling.
2. Follow the tapping script on the next page. Feel free to change my words to describe how you're feeling more accurately.
3. Rate the level of your anxiety and where you feel it in your body again on the same scale.
4. If it hasn't gone down, check the Troubleshooting chapter on page 259 to find out what to do next.
5. Think of one thing you're grateful for today and bask in your appreciation of it for a few moments.

Optional Extras for Maximum Benefit

6. Repeat the tapping script as many times as you have time for (and once is better than never!) for with the aim of reducing the intensity to 0.
7. Do one small, practical and manageable thing today that helps you manage better when an anxiety-provoking situation arises.
8. Write down your reflections in your journal or workbook.
9. Share with the Facebook support group:
    * how anxiety affects you and your parenting
    * what came up for you during the tapping today
    * what action you're going to take today to help you manage better when an anxiety-provoking situation arises
    * one thing you're grateful for today

10. Read a few of the other mums' comments and share some encouragement, support or inspiration to help you and your tribe members stay on track.
11. Glance at your Blissful Day visualisation to keep it fresh and alive in your mind – keep it somewhere easy to see, such as on the wall in the loo, on your phone, in your purse, by your bed, etc.

Day 22: Anxiety – tapping script

Side of hand: Even though I feel anxious, and I feel it in my [state part of body, or guess if you can't identify it], I acknowledge that this is how I'm feeling right now.
Even though I feel anxious about so many things, I accept myself and these feelings.
Even though I feel anxious and sometimes I don't even know why, I'm open to the possibility of being curious about this feeling and what I can learn from it.

Top of head: I'm acknowledging this anxious feeling.
Eyebrow: I'm noticing where I feel it in my [state part of body, or guess if you can't identify it].
Side of eye: I'm anxious about my [children, health, money, relationship, work, home, family etc].
Under eye: I'm allowing this feeling to be here now.
Under nose: I'm allowing myself to be present with this anxious feeling that I've been pushing away.
Chin: Maybe this anxiety is caused by things my mind can't control.
Collarbone: I choose to observe these anxious thoughts.
Under arm: I am not my thoughts.

Top of head: I am not my mind.
Eyebrow: As I become more aware of myself, I come into the present.
Side of eye: The future hasn't happened yet.
Under eye: The past is gone.
Under nose: This is the only moment that counts.
Chin: I choose to breathe into this moment.

Collarbone:	As I become more aware of this moment, I choose to infuse it with peace.
Under arm:	I'm noticing how my [state part of body experiencing the anxiety or guess if you can't identify it] is feeling now.
Top of head:	I'm breathing ease into the parts of me that are holding this anxious feeling.
Eyebrow:	I choose to infuse peace into all the anxious areas of my life.
Side of eye:	I choose to infuse peace into my [children, health, money, relationships etc].
Under eye:	As I do this, I notice my body relax.
Under nose:	Every cell is relaxing.
Chin:	My mind is relaxing.
Collarbone:	My feelings are easing.
Under arm:	I'm open to the possibility of having an anxiety-free day today.
Chest:	[taking a deep breath] Transform.

Day 23

Mothers' guilt

'I was struggling to remain calm and unagitated on the school run as my children were pushing my buttons with noise, preoccupation and general unwillingness to do anything that felt like cooperation. Everything felt like a fight. They were engrossed in their computer game, oblivious to my need to get them to school and me to work on time. I had woken up exhausted and was feeling like I was losing it. But I caught myself just in time. In the past I would have screamed at them and then felt so bad about it. Instead I said 'RIGHT! Let's stop. I'm overwhelmed. I need to do some tapping.' So I sat right there in the car (before I started driving!), and tapped on how I was feeling. They were ignoring me and arguing in the back. I tapped on everything I was feeling, adding observations about what they were doing into the tapping. Slowly the tapping and their activities merged into one and we all dissolved into giggles and set off to school!' Marina

Just a week to go now!

When the mums doing the online challenge completed the form you filled in on Day 3 about the consequences of not changing, one of the negative emotions that they said was holding them back most was guilt. Just under half of them rated their guilt at 7 or over.

Guilt about being a shouty, grumpy or unhappy mum, guilt that their children would grow up with the same issues they have, guilt about not setting a good example, guilt that their partner is having to put up with their stress, and more…

Mothers' guilt can start as soon as you know you're pregnant and try to eat the right foods when you're craving junk food or coffee, try to think positive thoughts when you're feeling crap or too exhausted to exercise, 'fail' to have a natural birth, or are unable to breastfeed.

As a community of mothers, we don't help the situation with our judgment of those who cannot or choose not to make what we consider the 'correct' or 'best' choices or decisions for their babies. When we feel guilty as mums we often overcompensate for our actions. Some of us continuously try to make up to our children for a 'bad' birth or our inability to breastfeed. If instead we can find compassion for ourselves and forgive ourselves, we can parent from a place of self-love, creating a deeper sense of connection to our children.

Our culture doesn't help mums by telling us we can have it all. Our role models are often celebrities who are able to spend time and money on their own and their children's appearance and seem to have the perfect work-life balance. The reality for most mums is very different: we're constantly trying to juggle too many balls, feeling there's never enough time and fire-fighting. The result can be that we feel guilty about not spending enough time with our children, and when we *are* with them we're not enjoying being with them because we're thinking about everything that needs to get done!

Now's the time to release all of that!

If you don't feel any guilt, that's great – take the opportunity to tap on any other negative emotion you may be feeling.

Thelma shared a typical example of her experience of guilt:

'Having rushed home, I started on dinner. It was a nightmare, as the children played up and didn't listen. My three-year-old went to bed all calm and I thought he was asleep. My seven-year-old watched TV while I was seeing my last client. Then both of them knocked on my door. I sent them out of my room. They returned a few minutes later, crying and playing up in front of my client. When I finished with my client there was a huge mess in the hallway where they'd thrown their toys down the stairs. I tried to put them to bed, but they just kept jumping about. All my anger has gone now, and but I'm left feeling so guilty because I have to live like this and juggle so much.' Thelma

Today's tapping script specifically addresses calming the mind when it's troubled by guilt about snapping at your children, not coping with the constant hamster wheel of motherhood, going back to work, not going back to work, sleep routines, baby feeding choices etc. Choose one aspect of motherhood that you feel guilty about for this next tapping script.

Action

1. Rate your level of guilt from 0 to 10, where at 0 you feel no guilt at all and at 10 you feel the most possible. If you can't relate to this issue choose a script from another day that's more relevant to how you're feeling.
2. Follow the tapping script on the next page. Feel free to change my words to describe how you're feeling more accurately.
3. Rate your level of guilt again from 0 to 10.
4. If it hasn't gone down, check the Troubleshooting chapter on page 259 to find out what to do next
5. Think of one thing you're grateful for today and bask in your appreciation of it for a few moments.

Optional Extras for Maximum Benefit

6. Repeat the tapping script as many times as you have time for (and once is better than never!) with the aim of reducing the intensity to 0.
7. Do one small, practical and manageable thing today that will help you to be kinder and more compassionate to yourself when you feel guilty, such as giving yourself a hug or telling yourself that you are a good-enough mum.
8. Write down your reflections in your journal or workbook.
9. Share with the Facebook support group:
    ❋ your relationship with guilt
    ❋ what came up for you during the tapping
    ❋ what action you're going to take today that will help you be kinder and more compassionate to yourself
    ❋ one thing you're grateful for
10. Read a few of the other mums' comments and share some encouragement, support or inspiration to help you and your tribe members stay on track.

11. Glance at your Blissful Day visualisation to keep it fresh and alive in your mind – keep it somewhere easy to see, such as on the wall in the loo, on your phone, in your purse, by your bed, etc.

Day 23: Mothers' guilt – tapping script

Side of hand: Even though I have this guilty feeling, I acknowledge this feeling just as it is.

Even though I feel guilty about things I should have done but haven't, I deeply and completely accept and forgive myself.

Even though I feel guilty about things I shouldn't have done but did, I choose to know that I'm a good mum anyway.

Top of head: I'm acknowledging this feeling of guilt.

Eyebrow: I'm feeling guilty about things I've done that that I shouldn't have done.

Side of eye: I'm feeling guilty about things I didn't do that I should have done.

Under eye: I'm feeling guilty about things that have happened to my children.

Under nose: I'm feeling guilty about things that haven't happened to my children.

Chin: I feel guilty about the way I've parented in the past.

Collarbone: I'm allowing all these memories of guilt to come into my awareness now.

Under arm: By acknowledging these memories I can start releasing this feeling now.

Top of head: I allow this feeling of guilt to be fully present.

Eyebrow: I allow this feeling of guilt to be present in my body.

Side of eye: I'm open to the possibility of releasing this feeling and letting it go.

Under eye: Feeling guilt doesn't make me a better mother.

Under nose:	Feeling guilt doesn't make me a better person.
Chin:	Punishing myself keeps me a prisoner of my own feelings.
Collarbone:	I choose to allow myself to acknowledge the guilt that I've been pushing away.
Under arm:	In the past it's been too uncomfortable to allow myself to feel it.
Top of head:	I'm open to the possibility of having compassion for myself and my feelings of guilt.
Eyebrow:	I choose to know and trust that I've always done the best I could with the resources I had at the time.
Side of eye:	I'm open to the possibility of sending love to the part of me that feels this guilt.
Under eye:	I wonder what kind of mum I would be if I didn't feel this guilt.
Under nose:	I choose to release the need to overcompensate for my guilty feelings.
Chin:	I choose to breathe compassion into the areas of my body that are feeling the guilt.
Collarbone:	I choose to replace my guilt with self-compassion.
Under arm:	I choose to replace my guilt with self-love.
Chest:	[taking a deep breath] Transform.

Day 24

Is your baby or your to-do list keeping you up at night?

'What a lovely way to end the 30 days with having had a good night's sleep, as my daughter slept for 11 hours last night. I'm glad to have taken part and been introduced to tapping. I feel I have definitely benefited from this and understand how important it is to have a few minutes out to myself. I'll be taking this forward with me. I also think I'm communicating better with my husband rather than acting like a robot and just getting on with everything, duties that can be shared. I want to continue to feel calm around my daughter and enjoy our first year together before I go back to work. This has been a wonderful opportunity.'
Martina

You're so close to the end of the challenge now. Keep up the great work!

One of the biggest challenges for mums is getting enough sleep.

The main reasons for lack of sleep are overthinking, and children not sleeping.

Getting a baby to sleep through the night is one of the biggest challenges a new mother in our culture faces, not only because she suffers from sleep deprivation and pressure from other mums or family members but also because it's considered normal for babies to sleep through the night.

Sleep deprivation is a form of torture. The sleep-deprived mother is more prone to depression, which itself can prevent her sleeping even when she has the opportunity. A sleep-deprived mother will do virtually anything to get her baby to sleep so that she can sleep herself.

In our culture we live in nuclear families without grandmothers, sisters or aunts on hand to help out. Women aren't designed to take on the task of looking after a baby single handed 24/7, so it's not surprising that there's so much peer pressure and emphasis on getting the baby to sleep through the night. Sharing the job of rearing a child with not just the father but others too can reduce feelings of overwhelm, exhaustion and loneliness, but it isn't easy to find a supportive community given how our society is structured.

Questions to consider are:

* Is it normal for a baby to sleep through the night?
* Do you normally sleep through the night yourself?
* Do you go to the loo in the night?
* Do you wake up periodically?
* Do you fall asleep again immediately, or do you lie awake for a while?
* Do you struggle to fall asleep in the first place?
* What are your beliefs about sleep?
* What did you learn about sleep when you were a child?
* Are you afraid of the dark?
* What attitude do you want your baby to have about sleep?

The answers to these questions could provide clues about your child's sleep challenges. How do the answers to these questions make you feel? If the feelings are negative, rate them on a scale from 0 to 10. You may like to incorporate some of the answers into the next tapping script to best represent what you are feeling.

If you struggle with sleep because your baby wakes you up, there's a video addressing this at Frazzledtofabulous.com/Bonus. Here's some lovely feedback that I've received from mums who watched it:

> 'Looked at your video tapping to help my baby sleep... Tapped with you... And my little toddler slept through the night! So today I salute you for helping me create a shift in my being and with my son! Jolie

> Oh my! Before bed last night I looked at and copied both of your EFT videos and oh my goodness... both two-year-old and I only woke once each! When I woke I didn't even bother to check the time, because rather than focusing on waking, I settled myself back and drifted off to sleep. Thank you so much, Tamara. Even

if it was just last night… but I'm open to miracles and will try tonight and going forward too xxxx Have a beautiful day x.' Kelly

Mums also suffer from sleep problems unconnected to their children. They may struggle with falling asleep, staying asleep and getting back to sleep, and can wake exhausted by their anxiety, worries, overthinking, and more. So here's a routine to help improve your sleep – this one can be done before bed!

Action

1. Rate how you feel about the quality of your sleep from 0 (great sleep – it's not a problem!) to 10 (worst sleep ever). If you can't relate to this issue choose a script from another day that's more relevant to how you're feeling.

2. Follow the tapping script on the next page. Feel free to change my words to describe how you're feeling more accurately.

3. Rate how you feel about the quality of your sleep again from 0 to 10.

4. If it hasn't gone down, check the Troubleshooting chapter on page 259 to find out what to do next.

5. Think of one thing you're grateful for today and bask in your appreciation of it for a few moments.

Optional Extras for Maximum Benefit

6. Repeat the tapping script as many times as you have time for (and once is better than never!) with the aim of reducing the intensity to 0.

7. Do one small, practical and manageable thing today to create better sleep for yourself.

8. Write down your reflections in your journal or workbook.

9. Share with the Facebook support group:
   - ❀ your relationship with sleep
   - ❀ what came up for you during the tapping
   - ❀ what action you're going to take today to create better sleep for yourself
   - ❀ one thing you're grateful for

10. Read a few of the other mum's comments and share some encouragement, support or inspiration to help you and your tribe members stay on track.

11. Glance at your Blissful Day visualisation to keep it fresh and alive in your mind – keep it somewhere easy to see, such as on the wall in the loo, on your phone, in your purse, by your bed, etc.

Day 24: Is your baby or your to-do list keeping you up at night? – tapping script

Side of hand: Even though I can't get to sleep or stay asleep, I acknowledge myself and this sleep problem.

Even though not sleeping well makes me feel exhausted and I can't focus properly, I accept myself just as I am.

Even though I can't remember the last time I woke up feeling refreshed, I choose to know that the more I tap the calmer I become, and the calmer I become the better I sleep.

Top of head: Not being able to sleep is the story of my life.

Eyebrow: I spend the night thinking, worrying and feeling anxious.

Side of eye: My to-do list keeps spinning round in my head.

Under eye: I keep mulling things over in my head.

Under nose: Maybe my baby or my children wake me up and I can't get back to sleep.

Chin: It makes me feel [tired, frustrated, fed up etc].

Collarbone: It feels like a never-ending spiral.

Under arm: I dream of a good night's sleep!

Top of head: I dream of waking refreshed and full of energy.

Eyebrow: I wish I could be raring to go when I wake up!

Side of eye: I wonder what it would be like to sleep well and wake up feeling rejuvenated.

Under eye: Is it possible to feel refreshed even if I don't sleep well?

Under nose: I'm open to the possibility of feeling relaxed when I lie down in bed.

Chin: I'm open to feeling grateful for the warmth and comfort of my bed.

Collarbone: I choose to allow my mind to soften as my head touches the pillow.

Under arm: And if I find myself awake in the night, maybe I can tap myself back to sleep…

Top of head: If I wake in the night, I'm open to allowing my body to relax.

Eyebrow: I choose to know that it's possible to fall back into a deep sleep.

Side of eye: I choose to know that it's possible to wake up refreshed in the morning even if my sleep's been interrupted.

Under eye: I'm open to the possibility of infusing tonight with deep, refreshing sleep.

Under nose: I choose to infuse my bed and my duvet with deep, relaxing energy.

Chin: I send my children deep, refreshing sleep energy.

Collarbone: I'm open to the possibility of all of us falling asleep at the right time tonight.

Under arm: I'm open to the possibility of all of us waking up at the right time tomorrow, feeling great!

Chest: [taking a deep breath] Transform.

Day 25

Waking up having to hit the ground running

'I'd never experienced tapping before and I can't believe that after a whole day of feeling that I could hardly keep my eyes open, I'm now feeling completely relaxed and energised, with no usual evening back pain.' Nathalie

I'm so happy to see you here again today!

So many mums struggle with the morning run. Perhaps you can relate to the following scenario:

You overslept because you only dropped off in the early hours, having spent the rest of the night worrying about how you were going to get it all done today. You rushed your children to get ready for school and lost your temper. You had a near-miss in traffic on the way to school because the children were arguing in the back of the car. You arrived at school stressed and irritated, and your youngest asked you if you still loved him. You arrived at work late, still carrying the guilt and stress of the morning run.

What if your day could start like this instead?

You wake up in the night thinking about your to-do list and spend two minutes tapping, which sends you back to sleep. On waking in the morning you spend another two minutes tapping to set you up for the day. When you feel yourself getting into an argument with one of your children you pop into the loo to tap. Two minutes

later you've regained your calm and returned to your child, feeling calm and centred, to deal with the situation in hand. On the way to school your children start arguing, so you remind them of their tapping fingers and soon they're chatting happily again. You arrive at school happy and relaxed, give your children big hugs, tell them you love them and drive off to work ready for your day ahead.

Get some inspiration from with the tapping video on waking up and hitting the ground running at Frazzledtofabulous.com/Bonus.

Action

1. Notice how you feel when you wake up in the morning and rate it from 0 to 10, with 0 calm, peaceful and light, and 10 the worst you could feel in terms of exhaustion, grumpiness, irritation, panic, etc. If you can't relate to this issue choose a script from another day that's more relevant to how you're feeling.

2. Follow the tapping script on the next page. Feel free to change my words to describe how you're feeling more accurately.

3. Rate how you feel now about waking up in the morning on the same scale.

4. If it hasn't gone down, check the Troubleshooting chapter on page 259 to find out what to do next.

5. Think of one thing you're grateful for today and bask in your appreciation of it for a few moments.

Optional Extras for Maximum Benefit

6. Repeat the tapping script as many times as you have time for (and once is better than never!) with the aim of reducing the intensity to 0.

7. Do one small, practical and manageable thing today to create an easier morning routine.

8. Write down your reflections in your journal or workbook.

9. Share with the Facebook support group:
   - ❋ how you feel about your morning routine
   - ❋ what came up for you during the tapping
   - ❋ what action you're going to take today to create an easier morning routine
   - ❋ one thing you're grateful for

10. Read a few comments from the other mums and share some encouragement, support or inspiration to help you and the members of your tribe to stay on track.

11. Glance at your Blissful Day visualisation to keep it fresh and alive in your mind – keep it somewhere easy to see, such as on the wall in the loo, on your phone, in your purse, by your bed, etc.

Day 25: Waking up having to hit the ground running – tapping script

Side of hand: Even though I wake up in the morning and have to hit the ground running, this is how my life is right now.

Even though I don't sleep well and wake up exhausted, I'm open to the possibility of knowing that it doesn't have to be this way, even in my current situation.

Even though there's so much to do in the morning, it's so stressful and seems never-ending, I choose to know and trust that there's another way.

Top of head: It's stressful getting myself and my children ready in the morning.
Eyebrow: I get impatient and then I feel guilty.
Side of eye: I'm overwhelmed at how much there is to do in such a short time.
Under eye: I often wake up too exhausted to think straight.
Under nose: I reach for coffee or sugar to keep me awake.
Chin: It feels like a vicious circle.
Collarbone: It feels like there's no give in my situation.
Under arm: I'm noticing where I feel all this exhaustion and stress in my body right now.

Top of head: Maybe I can let some of this stress go now.
Eyebrow: I wonder what I could change in my morning routine.
Side of eye: I wonder if I can still find some ease in my morning routine even if I feel exhausted.

Under eye:	I'm open to this possibility, even if I don't know how it could come about.
Under nose:	I breathe peace into my morning routine.
Chin:	I breathe ease into my morning routine.
Collarbone:	I breathe energy into my morning routine.
Under arm:	I breathe love into my morning routine.
Top of head:	I'm open to new possibilities.
Eyebrow:	I'm open to finding another way of being.
Side of eye:	I'm open to feeling good even when I wake up exhausted.
Under eye:	I'm open to feeling calm even when I have so much to do in such a short time.
Under nose:	I'm open to feeling patient even when my children are uncooperative.
Chin:	I'm open to finding an easy, natural flow to my mornings.
Collarbone:	I'm open to being unexpectedly surprised at how well my day can flow.
Under arm:	I'm open to magic and miracles for myself and my children.
Chest:	[taking a deep breath] Transform.

Day 26

Are you present with your children?

'After doing the tapping I feel more focused on preparing for school by pacing myself and the children, I have more patience with myself, making my needs important, and I'm feeling less stressed and more confident about trusting my own instincts.'
Yvonne

Young children change every day: there are so many 'firsts'! I remember when we took our daughter abroad for the first time when she was less than a year old. It was such a delight watching her experience sand, exploring the texture with her fingers and then her mouth. As they get older these firsts become rarer. I was delighted to share the awe and wonder my daughter experienced on her first visit to a rainforest – something she'd been wanting to do for many years – the year she finished her GCSEs.

When we're busy in our minds we can miss these unrepeatable moments. You never get that time back. This is the *only* moment there is. Your children are at the stage they are *right now*. They're continuously changing. Seize *this* moment and don't miss the gift of seeing them grow because you were too busy on your phone (I'm guilty of this myself sometimes)!

To be present with our children we need to learn to be present with ourselves. I remember thinking a few months ago about how all-consuming my phone had become – so I did an experiment, consciously deciding not to check it in every spare moment, such as in the car on the way to the cinema (I wasn't driving), waiting in line for cinema tickets and waiting for the film to start. Instead, I spent more time talking to my family and noticing my surroundings. This in turn helped me feel more present, focused and connected with my family and in turn they felt heard and appreciated.

But first we need to become more present with ourselves. Today we'll be tapping on becoming more present with ourselves so that we can be more present with our children.

Action

1. Rate how your connection with one of your children feels from 0 to 10, where at 0 you feel completely disconnected and at 10 you're feeling totally connected.
2. Follow the tapping script on the next page. If you can't relate to my words change them to match what you're feeling more accurately.
3. Rate your feeling of connection with your child again on the same scale.
4. If it hasn't gone up, check the Troubleshooting chapter on page 259 to find out what to do next.
5. Think of one thing that you're grateful for today and bask in your appreciation of it for a few moments.

Optional Extras for Maximum Benefit

6. Repeat the tapping script as many times as you have time for (and once is better than never!) for with the aim of reducing the intensity to 0.
7. Do one small, practical and manageable thing today to connect with one or more of your children.
8. Write down your reflections in your journal or workbook.
9. Share with the Facebook support group:
   - how you feel about your connection with your children
   - what came up for you during the tapping
   - what action you're going to take today to increase your connection to your children
   - one thing you're grateful for
10. Read a few comments from the other mums and share some encouragement, support or inspiration to help you and your tribe members stay on track.

11. Glance at your Blissful Day visualisation to keep it fresh and alive in your mind – keep it somewhere easy to see, such as on the wall in the loo, on your phone, in your purse, by your bed, etc.

Day 26: Are you present with your children? – tapping script

Side of hand: Even though my scattered mind stops me being present with my children, I acknowledge my mind and my lack of presence.

Even though I feel guilty when I'm not present with my children, I choose to know that I'm doing the best I can.

Even though sometimes part of me finds it easier when I'm not around them, I accept all parts of myself.

Top of head: I wish I could be more present with my children and let go of the thoughts in my head.

Eyebrow: I wish the time I spend with my children could be more enjoyable.

Side of eye: I allow myself to acknowledge any negative feelings I have about how present I am with my children.

Under eye: Maybe I can have compassion for myself for having those feelings.

Under nose: I'm open to the possibility of releasing some of these feelings now.

Chin: I wonder if I can release any guilt, stress, anxiety or overwhelm.

Collarbone: I wonder if I can let go of some of the cluttered thoughts in my mind that stop me being present.

Under arm: I acknowledge my lack of presence when I'm with my children with compassion.

Top of head: I wonder if I can learn to accept and forgive myself.

Eyebrow:	I wonder if I can learn to trust that I'm doing the best I can.
Side of eye:	I choose to acknowledge that I have a lot on my plate right now.
Under eye:	I choose to send compassion to the mum that I am right now.
Under nose:	I choose to acknowledge the times when I am present with my children.
Chin:	I choose to know that I'm a good enough mum just as I am.
Collarbone:	I choose to remember that my children love me.
Under arm:	I'm open to the possibility of sending myself love just as I am.
Top of head:	Maybe I can create a rainbow of love connecting my heart to my children's hearts.
Eyebrow:	I choose to know and trust that this rainbow of love is flowing in abundance.
Side of eye:	It flows when we're together and when we're apart.
Under eye:	It flows even when I'm with them but my mind is on other things.
Under nose:	I'm open to finding an easy way to connect with my children today.
Chin:	I'm connecting with my children whether we're together or apart.
Collarbone:	I choose to send them confidence, joy and peace.
Under arm:	I'm sending them love wherever they are.
Chest:	[taking a deep breath] Transform.

Day 27

Creating your Blissful Day revisited

'The challenge helped me to focus on myself at a difficult time and I have let myself be supported and encouraged throughout the programme. I feel more calm and am able to feel positive about the future. This will impact on my relationships with my husband, children and grandchildren.' Jen

Welcome back to your Blissful Day tapping session. How is your vision of your Blissful Day evolving? Have you noticed aspects of your visualisation seeping into your daily life? Has what you want for your Blissful Day changed? Has visualising it become easier or harder?

If you're struggling to connect with your vision because it's so far from your current reality, don't worry. The key is to connect with the feelings and emotions you would experience during your Blissful Day. For example if you're a single mum working full-time with no support, and your vision is of lying on a beach on a tropical island all by yourself, that might be hard to imagine. But if you can imagine how it would make you feel – eg relaxed, calm, blissful, peaceful, grateful etc – could you allow yourself to connect with those emotions? If you could, where would you feel them in your body? If you don't know, just guess. What would the physical sensation be in that part of your body? Again, if you don't know, just guess. And if you knew what colours those emotions would be, what would they be? Use these colours, feelings and physical sensations to support your tapping today.

Carol shared how on the day she was doing the Blissful Day tapping she had an early start at 5:00am with a busy day ahead. She made breakfast and then went back to bed to do the tapping while her parents minded her daughter. She reflected: 'Initially I thought there was no way I could achieve my Blissful Day, given that I'd be working all day and night. But as I got going I realised that having a sense of feeling my Blissful Day was all I needed to get me through. I began to feel lighter and softer throughout the tapping session.'

Action

1. Think of your Blissful Day and rate your level of joy, excitement, peace, happiness or other positive emotion on a scale from 0 to 10. This time 0 represents no joy or other positive emotion at all and 10, the most possible, so the tapping will increase your positive feelings rather than reducing your negative ones.
2. Follow the tapping script on the next page. Feel free to change my words to describe how you're feeling more accurately.
3. Focus on your Blissful Day again and rate your positive emotion again – it should have gone up…
4. If it hasn't gone up, check the Troubleshooting chapter on page 259 to find out what to do next.
5. Think of one thing that you're grateful for today and bask in your appreciation of it for a few moments.

Optional Extras for Maximum Benefit

6. Repeat the tapping script as many times as you have time for (and once is better than never!) with the aim of raising the level of your chosen positive emotion to 10.
7. Do one small, practical and manageable thing today to help you experience more joy.
8. Write down your reflections in your journal or workbook.
9. Share with the Facebook support group:
    * how you feel about your Blissful Day
    * what came up for you during the tapping
    * what action you're going to take today to create more joy
    * one thing you're grateful for
10. Read a few comments from other mums in the Facebook support group and share some encouragement, support or inspiration to help you and the members of your tribe to stay on track.

11. Glance at your Blissful Day visualisation to keep it fresh and alive in your mind – keep it somewhere easy to see, such as on the wall in the loo, on your phone, in your purse, by your bed, etc.

Day 27: Creating your Blissful Day revisited – tapping script

Side of hand: I choose to experience my Blissful Day energy no matter what's going on in my day and my life right now.

I'm connecting to the colour, feeling and sensation of my Blissful Day.

I choose to know and trust that the colour, feeling and sensation of my Blissful Day are infusing every cell of my body.

Top of head: I'm infusing today with blissful energy.

Eyebrow: I'm infusing the colour, feeling and sensation of blissful energy into every cell of my body.

Side of eye: I'm letting go of any remaining resistance to experiencing even more blissful energy.

Under eye: I'm infusing blissful energy into every fibre of my being.

Under nose: I'm noticing how this energy feels in my body.

Chin: I'm noticing how this energy feels in my mind.

Collarbone: I'm noticing my feelings associated with my Blissful Day energy.

Under arm: I'm infusing positive feelings and blissful energy into this moment.

Top of head: I'm infusing my positive feelings and blissful energy into the rest of the day.

Eyebrow: I'm infusing my positive feelings and blissful energy into my home.

Side of eye: I'm infusing my positive feelings and blissful energy into my children.

Under eye:	I'm infusing my positive feelings and blissful energy into my parenting.
Under nose:	[if relevant] I'm infusing my positive feelings and blissful energy into my relationship with my partner.
Chin:	I'm infusing my positive feelings and blissful energy into my work.
Collarbone:	I'm infusing my positive feelings and blissful energy into my friendships.
Under arm:	I'm infusing my positive feelings and blissful energy into my health.
Top of head:	I'm infusing my positive feelings and blissful energy into my finances.
Eyebrow:	I'm infusing my positive feelings and blissful energy into my parents.
Side of eye:	I'm infusing my positive feelings and blissful energy into my me-time.
Under eye:	I'm infusing my positive feelings and blissful energy into my past.
Under nose:	I'm infusing my positive feelings and blissful energy into my future.
Chin:	I'm infusing my positive feelings and blissful energy into my children's futures.
Collarbone:	I'm infusing my positive feelings and blissful energy into every aspect of my life.
Under arm:	I'm infusing my life with an abundance of magic and miracles.
Chest:	[taking a deep breath] Transform.

Silva and Bronte's story

Three generations of EFT

Silva: I was introduced to Tamara's EFT work with mums whilst training to become a practitioner and have been using it with my family ever since.

As a grandmother and great-grandmother I have found EFT to be an absolute boon, from using it to support my granddaughter in giving birth to her daughter (she actually gave birth on my living room floor in the most easy and natural delivery) to using what is known as surrogate tapping for two of my grandchildren.

(See page 241 for information on surrogate tapping and how to do it.)

One of my granddaughters had a horrendous Year 7 at school and was at the point of breaking down with unhappiness and not being able to cope. I did 28 days of surrogate tapping for her, every day tapping on various issues around her distress. The outcome was more than I could have hoped for and she went into Year 8 feeling really confident, gained new friends, and is making a point of befriending the new Year 7 intake!

After I did surrogate tapping for my 16-year-old grandson there was an obvious breakthrough, and he actually started to talk to his parents about his feelings and improvement in his college work.

One of my granddaughters, Bronte, trained as an EFT practitioner as well. She took part in Tamara's 30-Day Challenge and reported at the end: 'Tapping every day is having such an impact on every area of my life. I've just realised I can't remember the last time I felt nauseous (been suffering with this five days out of seven for about eight months) and I've been changing binbags for the last two weeks. This may seem absurd to some, but bins were a no-go area for me just a few weeks ago. And I haven't even tapped on those issues.'

Bronte has also been using EFT with her daughters:

My two-year-old scratched my other daughter (aged 5). There was no retaliation or complaining to me. Before I could say anything, she very calmly picked up her little sister's hand and surprised me by saying 'Even though I've hurt my sister and might feel a bit bad about it, I'm still a great kid'. So I'm finding that EFT is only helping her not only to deal with her own issues but to think about others' feelings too.

Day 28

Catch up and recap

'Feeling that I have really reconnected with myself and feeling so much brighter over the last few weeks. At long last I'm really happy with how I'm listening/being in touch and accepting what is going on in my body.' Debbie

You'll be pleased to know that today's a catch-up day! You've put in a lot of effort to get this far. Every time you tap, you release a bit more of the stress and overwhelm that got you to pick up this book in the first place, creating more positive change for yourself and your family. And you're nearly there – I'm so excited for you!

You started the week with releasing anxiety and guilt. When I ran the challenge online, mums reported in the questionnaire that after stress and overwhelm, anxiety, followed closely by guilt, were the strongest emotions that bothered them. On the scale from 0 to 10 their average ratings were 6.9 for anxiety and 6.4 for guilt.

From there you continued with some tapping to support better sleep so that you can start the day more positively even when you're tired. The next day you tapped on having a better connection to your children and being more present with yourself so that you can be more present with them. As usual, you finished the week with some Blissful Day tapping.

I'm so pleased that bit by bit you're reducing the levels of these negative emotions for yourself so that you can create a calmer and more harmonious environment for your whole family.

Action

1. If you're up to speed and want to create more momentum and do some more tapping, repeat one of the tapping scripts from previous days or simply have a rest day.
2. If you feel you'd benefit from seeing tapping in action, check out the Frazzled to Fabulous Membership Club at Frazzledtofabulous. com/Bonus.
3. Do one thing for yourself today. Now that you've been tapping for almost a month, consider how, with minimal effort, you could arrange an hour or even half a day for yourself doing something you love. It could be going to a yoga class, meeting a friend for a walk, or sitting in a coffee shop reading a book. Take one small action today towards making that your reality.

Day 29

I am enough

'Before doing this challenge my rating of enoughness would have been so low; today before tapping it was about a 6, and after tapping it was an 8. I'm a perfectionist, so feeling I'm enough is quite tricky. As a mother and wife I have high expectations about how I should behave and what I should be achieving, but since doing this challenge that feeling of not being enough has reduced dramatically.' Sarah

Only two days to go. Go YOU! You're amazing.

Do you feel and know that you're enough just as you are? Or are you self-critical, do you judge yourself, not make yourself a priority and lack self-belief?

A few months ago I was motivated to create a beautiful flyer, designed by my daughter, with the affirmation 'I'm enough' on it. When the package arrived from the printers I absolutely adored it and just looking at it made me feel so good. And then it dawned on me – I'd made the flyers for myself! I needed to hear and know that I'm enough! So I tapped on this and am now feeling stronger and stronger in my sense of self and enoughness. And this is what I want for you too.

You ARE enough. You are MORE than enough. And your children love you, despite your impatience and your imperfection. Now let's get tapping on that to increase your sense of enoughness!

Action

1. Rate your belief that you're enough just the way you are from 0 to 10, where at 0 you don't believe it at all and at 10 you totally believe it.
2. Follow the tapping script on the next page. Feel free to change my words to describe how you're feeling more accurately.
3. Rate your level of belief that you're enough again.
4. If it hasn't gone up, check the Troubleshooting chapter on page 259 to find out what to do next.
5. Think of one thing that you're grateful for today and bask in your appreciation of it for a few moments.

Optional Extras for Maximum Benefit

6. Repeat the tapping script as many times as you have time for (and once is better than never!) with the aim of increasing your belief to 10.
7. Do one small, practical and manageable thing today to create a stronger sense of knowing that you're enough just as you are.
8. Write down your reflections in your journal or workbook.
9. Share with the Facebook support group:
    ❋ your sense of enoughness
    ❋ what came up for you during the tapping
    ❋ what action you're going to take today to create a stronger sense of knowing you're enough
    ❋ one thing you're grateful for
10. Read a few of the other mum's comments and share some encouragement, support or inspiration to help you and the members of your tribe to stay on track.
11. Glance at your Blissful Day visualisation to keep it fresh and alive in your mind – keep it somewhere easy to see, such as on the wall in the loo, on your phone, in your purse, by your bed, etc.

Day 29: I am enough – tapping script

Side of hand: Even though part of me feels that I'm not enough just as I am, I acknowledge that part of me with love.

Even though part of me doesn't feel that I'm enough just as I am, I'm open to the possibility of letting some of that feeling go.

Even though part of me feels that I'm not enough, I choose to infuse that part of me with an abundance of 'enoughness' energy.

Top of head: I'm noticing that 'I'm not enough' feeling.

Eyebrow: Maybe it's been there a long time.

Side of eye: Maybe it's always been there.

Under eye: Maybe it's because of things that have happened in the past.

Under nose: Maybe it's what I was told as a child.

Chin: Maybe it's what I've experienced.

Collarbone: I'm allowing that 'I'm not enough' feeling to be here now.

Under arm: I'm allowing myself to fully feel that 'I'm not enough' feeling.

Top of head: By feeling it fully I can start releasing it.

Eyebrow: When I release it I can make way for the 'I am enough' feeling to arise within me.

Side of eye: I'm open to the possibility of letting go of some of that 'I'm not enough' feeling.

Under eye: I choose to send love to the part of me that believes that I'm not enough.

Under nose: I choose to send compassion to that part of me.

Chin: I choose to send acceptance to that part of me.

Collarbone:	I choose to send healing to that part of me.
Under arm:	I choose to guess how it would feel to know that I am enough.
Top of head:	I choose to guess where I would feel that in my body.
Eyebrow:	I choose to imagine what the sensation would be in that part of my body.
Side of eye:	I choose to imagine how it would feel if I truly believed that I am enough.
Under eye:	I choose to infuse my cells with 'I am enough' energy now.
Under nose:	I choose to infuse every fibre of my being with 'I am enough' energy.
Chin:	I choose to infuse this moment with an abundance of 'I am enough' energy.
Collarbone:	I choose to infuse the rest of the day with an abundance of 'I am enough' energy.
Under arm:	I choose to infuse the whole of my life with an abundance of 'I am enough' energy.
Chest:	[taking a deep breath] Transform.

Day 30

Celebration

'During this challenge I have noticed lots of areas that contributed to feeling a huge sense of stress, anger, failure and never enough time to achieve anything. I really cannot explain or understand how such a huge shift in my mental wellbeing has come about. I have found this experience so uplifting and feel so much happier than when I started this.' Sandra

Whoopee! YOU DID IT! 30 days, and here you are at the end. What an amazing journey! You're totally awesome. You've laid the foundations for incredible changes in your own and your children's life. I'm so proud and happy for you, and excited for your children, who are going to have a happier, calmer, more present mum. Get ready to CELEBRATE!

30 days ago you embarked on this journey. If you're like the mums who took part in the challenge online there will have been tears, laughter, giving up, starting again, frustration, successes, and everything in between. Hopefully you'll have seen some positive changes in yourself, from sleeping better to being more patient with your children, having more energy, and feeling lighter and happier.

On Day 3 of the challenge I asked you to complete a form rating your top challenges.

I would have given it to you on Day 1, but I didn't because I've learnt from experience that it can bring up low feelings. I didn't want you to give up before you got started. Giving you the questionnaire on Day 3 meant that you could start tapping to release any low feelings straight away.

When I ran the challenge online the ratings for all of the questions at the beginning of the challenge improved when I presented the questionnaire again at the end, with the greatest improvement (38–43 per cent) in anxiety, overwhelm, guilt, and 'how am I going to get it all done?'

When I ran this challenge for the first time I knew it would create great results for the mums involved. But what really surprised me were the unexpected positive side effects that they reported in all areas of their lives, even including their health, their relationships and their finances. And the best part is that the people around them

noticed the differences too. You can revisit some of their comments in the introduction.

So here we are at the end, and I'm going to ask you to fill in the questionnaire again and reflect on what's changed for you since Day 3.

Action

1. Complete the forms on page 221 and 222. Rate the intensity of the feelings and thoughts listed from 0 to 10, where 0 doesn't affect you at all and 10 has the greatest intensity possible. If you want to be accountable and you completed the Day 3 form online, you can access the Day 30 form at Frazzledtofabulous.com/Bonus.

2. Reflect on what's changed for you and the challenges that remain. Remember, Rome wasn't built in a day. Over the last 30 days you've laid the foundations for permanent change. Consider how you're going to take these new habits into the future. If you'd like support with this, check out the possibilities on Frazzledtofabulous.com/Bonus.

3. Do the Celebration tapping on page 223.

4. Go celebrate!!!

5. Think of one thing you're grateful for today and bask in your appreciation of it for a few moments.

Optional Extras for Maximum Benefit

6. Repeat the tapping script as many times as you have time for (and once is better than never!) with the aim of increasing the intensity of your celebration energy to 10.

7. Do one small, practical and manageable thing today to celebrate your successful completion of the challenge. It might be coffee with a friend, putting your favourite outfit on just because, or enjoying a takeaway with your partner…

8. Write down your reflections in your journal or workbook.

9. Share with the Facebook support group:
    * how you feel at the end of the challenge
    * anything that came up for you in the questionnaire
    * what action you're going to take today to celebrate your success
    * one thing you're grateful for

10. Read a few of the other mums' comments and share some encouragement, support or inspiration to help you and the members of your tribe stay on track.

11. Glance at your Blissful Day visualisation to keep it fresh and alive in your mind – keep it somewhere easy to see, such as on the wall in the loo, on your phone, in your purse, by your bed, etc.

Reflection:
How do you feel 30 days on?

Here are the top symptoms that that you rated at the beginning of the challenge. Rate how much each of them regularly affects you on a scale from 0 to 10, where 0 doesn't affect you at all and 10 affects you a lot or all the time. You can complete the questionnaire online at Frazzledtofabulous.com/Bonus or fill it out in the book, below.

Symptom	Rating (0-10)	Symptom	Rating (0-10)
Emotion		**Behaviour**	
Anger		Beating myself up for not saying NO	
Anxiety		Cravings – sugar, coffee, wine, cigarettes, etc	
Exhaustion		Letting people down	
Fear		Overcommitting	
Guilt		Not putting myself first	
Overthinking		There's always something more important than me	
Overwhelm		**Health challenges**	
Procrastination		Digestive problems	
Resentment		Headaches/migraines	
Stress		Period problems	
Add your own particular challenges here		Trouble sleeping	

Reflection Questions

	What are the biggest changes you've noticed in these areas of your life?	What would be the cost of not continuing the progress you've made with each of these?	How will you ensure that you can create and maintain the results you want?	What will you put in place to get you back on track when things go pear-shaped?
Your emotions				
Your thoughts				
Your children				
Your partner				
Your health				
Your work				
Your finances				
Your home				

Day 30: Celebration – tapping script

Side of hand: Even though I'm still a work in progress, I'm open to the possibility of celebrating the steps I've taken to change my life and the lives of my children.

Even though I'm still a work in progress, I choose to celebrate my successes along the way.

Even though I'll always be a work in progress, as life is about the journey, not the end result, I choose to enjoy the treasures along the way.

Top of head: Celebrating my successes.

Eyebrow: Celebrating all the new actions I've taken.

Side of eye: Celebrating all the new thoughts I've had.

Under eye: Celebrating the changes in my behaviour.

Under nose: Celebrating myself just the way I am.

Chin: Celebrating myself just the way I'm not!

Collarbone: Celebrating my children just the way they are.

Under arm: Celebrating my children just the way they're not.

Top of head: I choose to infuse every cell, atom and molecule with celebration energy.

Eyebrow: I choose to infuse every fibre of my being with celebration energy.

Side of eye: I choose to radiate that celebration energy back into my past.

Under eye: I choose to radiate that celebration energy into the rest of the day.

Under nose: I choose to radiate that celebration energy into my work.

Chin: I choose to radiate that celebration energy into my home.

Collarbone:	I choose to radiate that celebration energy into my children.
Under arm:	[if relevant] I choose to radiate that celebration energy into my partner.
Top of head:	I choose to radiate that celebration energy into my family relationships.
Eyebrow:	I choose to radiate that celebration energy into my relationships with my friends.
Side of eye:	I choose to radiate that celebration energy into my health.
Under eye:	I choose to radiate that celebration energy into every aspect of my life.
Under nose:	I choose to make my celebration energy even bigger and stronger.
Chin:	I choose to make my celebration energy even more vibrant and vivid.
Collarbone:	Infusing it into every aspect of my life.
Under arm:	I choose to infuse it into my long and happy future and for generations to come.
Chest:	[taking a deep breath] Transform.

Congratulations! You've come to the end of the 30-Day Challenge. I'd love to hear how you got on and with your permission share your story to inspire other mums; please email me at info@tamaradonn. com.

PART 3
Moving Forward

Introduction

So you've completed 30 days of tapping and perhaps you're wondering?

- 🌼 what next?
- 🌼 will the positive changes last?
- 🌼 what can I do to keep up the momentum?
- 🌼 how do I take this forward?
- 🌼 how can I use it with my children?

Keep watering your plant!

When you started reading this book you were probably feeling stressed, overwhelmed and exhausted. Perhaps you had no time for yourself and felt guilty because you were often impatient with your children. Maybe you felt a bit like this wilted plant, because you'd forgotten to keep yourself watered.

On each of the 30 days of this challenge I gave you a full watering can, and all you had to do was pour the water into your pot by creating five minutes for yourself to release your overwhelm, stress, procrastination, and more. The great news is that your plant is beginning to thrive! To keep it alive and thriving, you'll need to continue watering it every day.

How are you going to keep up the momentum that you've built up?

The key thing is to carry on doing it every day until it becomes as natural and automatic as brushing your teeth. It takes 30 days to create a new habit, so you've done the hard part already.

Support and accountability

Maintaining a daily habit is easier with friends or in a community. When you're supporting others and they're supporting you, you're more likely to keep up the good work. Can you get together with friends, create a group, do five minutes with other mums, meet up online with friends who live further away?

If you feel you would benefit from regular tapping videos and a support group to help keep you on track, do join the mums club at Frazzledtofabulous.com/Bonus.

What if I forget to tap?

You will! We all do. It's part of being human. What's important is what you do and tell yourself when you *do* forget. Usually it's because life has got in the way: you had a bad night; it's the end of term and there's so much to do and prepare before the holidays; one of your children got ill, or you were hit by some other curve ball! Just because you forgot to tap once, twice, or even for a week it doesn't mean you've failed or that you can't get back to it. The I've fallen behind section on page 264 will help you get back on track.

An accountability partner or group will support you greatly through these challenges.

I don't know what to tap on

If you don't know what to tap on, choose any of the topics in this book and follow the tapping script. If none of them resonate, pick any issue that's affecting you and tap on that, following the form of the tapping scripts in the book. If the words in the script don't match how you feel, replace them with your own. If you want to know more about how to do this see the Next steps section on page 253.

I want my fabulous feeling to be sustainable and grow

Coming back to the plant analogy, plants don't only need water. If your plant has never been repotted it can only grow and thrive so much before it needs attention. When you picked up this book you may have been familiar with EFT but wanted to be able to use it for yourself and with your family. Perhaps you want to take your parenting to the next level. Or you may be struggling in certain areas of your parenting – for example you may be committed to not doing what your parents did, only to hear your mum's words coming out of your mouth, or have outbursts of anger at your children that you feel guilty about – and you're ready to commit to releasing the root causes so that your parenting can be joyful and relaxed and you have a really great connection with your children.

Read the Digging deeper chapter on page 254 for more information on how to embed your tapping habit and take it to the next level.

Use EFT in times of stress

When EFT has truly become a habit, you'll find it easier and easier to turn to it as your go-to place in times of stress. Tapping has become so second-nature to me that my fingers automatically start tapping whenever I notice negative emotions arise. So you don't think I'm a complete nutter, I use points on the fingers that can be tapped on discreetly in public! You can learn these tapping points by downloading my free introductory How to Tap video or the free manual accessible on Frazzledtofabulous.com/Bonus.

> One parenting EFT success of mine happened when my daughter came home drunk one night and vomited into the compost bin. I could feel the disappointment and anger rising inside me. In that moment I knew that my attitude would not support the situation, so I removed myself for a couple of moments to defuse my negative emotions. As I tapped, I remembered the times I'd been drunk at her age and released my judgement of her. This helped me to empathise with her. When I returned, I was able to take care of her. In the morning she thanked me for being so kind and supportive. Had I taken out my anger on her I would only have pushed her away.

EFT can be used in so many different types of situations. I've already described in the Introduction how I used it when my mum fell and needed stitches at the A&E. Here are some other occasions when I've used EFT as my go-to place:

❋ to release pain in my vocal chords when joined a choir – I tell my story about this at Frazzledtofabulous.com/Bonus.

❋ when I was skiing with my husband and got stuck at the top of a mountain – he supported me down the hill by tapping with me to release my fears!

❋ when I was feeling nervous before performing in a show

❋ when I twisted my ankle
❋ with my daughter preparing her for GCSE exams
❋ when my daughter came home from school upset because she'd seen a dog being run over

Your children and EFT

Introduction

So many mums want to know how to use tapping with their children. EFT is a fantastic parenting tool, and I love using it with my daughter and on myself to help me get clarity when I'm struggling with how to parent her.

Here are some ideas of how you can use EFT to support your children:

* in difficult situations, eg when they're suffering from bullying, peer or academic pressure, have fallen and hurt themselves, sibling rivalry
* in the daily routine, eg getting up, going to bed, mealtimes
* to get free of bad habits, eg thumb-sucking, when eating, nail-biting
* to ease transitions, eg moving house, starting school, parents' divorce
* decision-making, eg about what to wear, whether or not to go to the party
* achieving goals, eg succeeding at exams and sports
* to empower them by helping them release negative emotions and instil new, positive feelings

More importantly, EFT can support you with your feelings about your child and with your parenting, whatever your style. Doing EFT on yourself is the starting point and the key to controlling your emotions. The calmer and the more grounded, stable and happy you are, the more present you'll be in your parenting and the more connected you'll be with your children – your relationship with them will be better and your parenting experience will be easier!

When my daugther was preparing for her exams, she gave them her all, spending whole days revising in the months leading up to them. Once the exams were over she went into an irritable and grumpy state, taking all her unravelling stress out on me. Although I understood why she was behaving like that, I was still upset. That evening I was able to tap and release my upset rather than carry it around, affecting our relationship.

Wording

When tapping with children it's important to use age-appropriate wording. 'I deeply and completely accept myself' may be beyond a younger child's comprehension. It's a good idea to simplify the language and make it relevant to them:

✽ Even though I feel bad that I don't want Katy to come over to play, I'm still a great kid
✽ Even though I'm struggling to get down to my revision, I'm okay anyway
✽ Even though I'm feeling sad, my mummy and daddy still love me

Four steps to tapping with children

You won't necessarily need all four of these steps, but always follow the ones you do use in this order. Sometimes the first one or two do the trick.

Step 1: Tap on how you feel

I can't emphasise the importance of this step enough. So many mums I know don't do it, and I can understand why. When your child is in pain or suffering it can feel unbearable: we're so inextricably linked to our children that when they suffer, we suffer too. We want to fix them so that we can stop suffering ourselves.

> Sandra contacted me when her daughter started biting her nails soon after she'd left her with a new babysitter, who'd told Sandra that her daughter hadn't settled well. I tapped with Sandra on how she felt about this: guilt about leaving her daughter, concern about the possible repercussions, and worry about the nail-biting. Sandra contacted me about a week after our session and told me that her daughter had stopped biting her nails.

Tapping on how you yourself feel about your child's situation can change the situation itself. I know that's hard to believe, but I encourage you to give it a go.

Tapping on how you feel, along with Step 2 on page 238, is particularly useful when your child is preverbal or doesn't want to tap for herself.

Exercise:

Think of something that bothers you about your child or your relationship with your child right now: for example she or he

- ❀ isn't making friends
- ❀ is spending too much time on social media
- ❀ doesn't sleep well at night
- ❀ has lots of tantrums
- ❀ is rude
- ❀ is a fussy eater
- ❀ doesn't seem to like you
- ❀ has issues with his/her body image

When you think about this issue, how does it make you feel?

1. Rate the feeling on a scale from 0 to 10, where 0 is calm, peaceful and light, and 10 is the most intense possible.
2. Follow the tapping script on the next page, remembering that I don't know your situation or your child: if my words don't match your feelings, situation or issue, change them to represent what feels true to you.
3. Rate the feeling again on the same scale.
4. Repeat as necessary until the feeling has dropped to 0.
5. If you don't have much time, just do as much as you can. One round is better than none!

Tapping script for accepting feelings about an issue with your child

Side of hand: Even though I feel [state emotion, or guess if you can't identify it] about [name the issue] with [child's name], I acknowledge my feelings about [child's name].

Even though I feel [state emotion, or guess if you can't identify it] and I can feel it in my [state part of body, or guess if you can't identify it], I accept myself and my feelings.

Even though [child's name] is going through this and it brings up difficult emotions for me, I'm here, and I'm doing the best I can.

Top of head: I acknowledge my [issue] with [child's name].

Eyebrow: It feels really difficult.

Side of eye: It makes me feel [emotion].

Under eye: I feel it in my [part of body].

Under nose: If that feeling had a colour it would be [state colour, or guess if you don't know].

Chin: If it had a shape, it would be [state shape, or guess if you don't know].

Collarbone: I choose to acknowledge this [colour, shape] in my [part of body, eg 'this blue ball in my chest'].

Under arm: Sometimes this feeling is so unbearable.

Top of head: If I could only change this situation for [child's name] I'd feel better.

Eyebrow: It doesn't make me a bad mum.

Side of eye: I'm tapping because I really care.

Under eye: I want the best for me, for [child's name] and our relationship.

Under nose:	So I'm bringing some compassion for myself into this situation.
Chin:	I choose to know and trust that I'm doing the best I can.
Collarbone:	I choose to know and trust that my best is good enough.
Under arm:	I'm open to the possibility of infusing myself, [child's name] and this situation with love and trust.
Chest:	[taking a deep breath] Transform.

Step 2: Send positive qualities to your child

This step can be done at any time, even if you don't have an issue with your child. I used it a lot when my daughter was doing her exams to send her ease, clarity, focus, success, knowledge etc. You can include whatever positive feelings you want your child to have. Here's an example tapping script to use as a starting point.

Tapping script for sending a child positive qualities

Side of hand: Sending [child's name] love.
Sending [child's name] trust.
Sending [child's name] joy.

Top of head: Sending [child's name] peace.
Eyebrow: Sending [child's name] good health.
Side of eye: Sending [child's name] confidence.
Under eye: Sending [child's name] ease.
Under nose: Sending [child's name] trust.
Chin: Sending [child's name] self-acceptance.
Collarbone: Sending [child's name] self-love.
Under arm: Sending [child's name] focus.

Top of head: Sending [child's name] kindness.
Eyebrow: Sending [child's name] the knowledge and feeling that s/he's loved.
Side of eye: Sending [child's name] energy.
Under eye: Sending [child's name] good sleep at night.
Under nose: Sending [child's name] the ability to make healthy eating choices.
Chin: Sending [child's name] safety.
Collarbone: Sending [child's name] an abundance of all of these qualities.
Under arm: Sending [child's name] magic and miracles.
Chest: [taking a deep breath] Transform.

Step 3: Tapping for your children

This step is particularly useful when your child is too young to talk or express his feelings, or doesn't want to tap himself. I don't recommend Step 3 before you have released your own upsetting feelings about your child or your situation first as described in Step 1. It is possible to miss out Step 2 but I personally love doing Step 2!

Tapping for your children is also known as surrogate tapping and involves tapping for your child as if you *are* your child. There are different schools of thought about whether it's ethical to tap on your child if you haven't first asked their permission to do so, and some people say it's manipulative to tap on a behaviour outcome that you want for your child when your child is resisting changing in this area. For example, if your child is trying to persuade you to get her an iPhone, or whatever the latest 'must-have' is, and you tap on her not wanting an iPhone, that could be considered manipulative.

I remember a situation that occurred when I was an inexperienced practitioner. A client wanted to do some surrogate tapping on her daughter, who was treating her granddaughter in a way that my client she felt was detrimental to the child. We tapped for her daughter to change, but could not get the intensity she was feeling down because it was my client's issue, not her daughter's. I gently suggested that we tap on how she felt about the fact that her daughter was not treating her granddaughter nicely, and she was able to access and release her feelings of anxiety, helplessness and fear for the future. She then felt a lot stronger in her position as both mother and grandmother, and more accepting of the situation. From this place of strength she was able to move on to surrogate tapping.

You can do surrogate tapping for children of any age. I have also helped mums to do surrogate tapping for babies in the womb. Read an example of this in the section During pregnancy on page 244.

How to do surrogate tapping

❋ Mentally step into your child's shoes and say 'I am [your child's name]'

❋ Tap as if you are your child, adapting the example tapping script on the next page, which can be used for any challenge your child is going through: feeling ill, sad, or angry, not feeding, suffering from an addiction, bullying or being bullied, etc.

❋ Repeat as many times as necessary

❋ At the end of the tapping session say 'I am me' and feel yourself back in your own shoes

Surrogate tapping script for a child

This is just an example. Adapt the wording to suit your child's age, situation and feelings.

Mentally step into your child's shoes and say 'I am [your child's name]'

Side of hand: Even though I'm feeling upset that [pet's name] died, I'm a great kid OR
Even though I'm feeling upset that [pet's name] died, I deeply and completely accept myself.
Even though I feel like it's my fault, maybe I didn't do anything wrong.
Even though I'm so sad, I'll always remember the fun times I had with [pet's name].

Top of head: Upset.
Eyebrow: Sad.
Side of eye: Missing [pet's name].
Under eye: I wish I could have him back.
Under nose: It's what happens,
Chin: I don't like it.
Collarbone: It feels like it's my fault.
Under arm: Feeling guilty.
Top of head: It's not my fault.
Eyebrow: It's nobody's fault.
Side of eye: Maybe I can remember the good things about him.
Under eye: This sadness in my body.
Under nose: Maybe I can let some of that sadness go.
Chin: And still remember [pet's name].
Collarbone: Maybe it's okay to feel sad sometimes.

Under arm: Maybe it's okay to feel sad because I'll feel better soon.

Chest: [taking a deep breath] Transform.

Say 'I am me' and feel yourself back in your own shoes.

Step 4: Tapping with your children

This is the section most mums are interested in. If you've jumped here first, please do read from the beginning of the section headed Your children and EFT on page 232 first for the best results. For age-appropriate EFT strategies, see the section on tapping for different age groups below.

It's easier to establish a tapping habit with younger children than with older ones. Once they're used to using it you can suggest they try it out when they fall over, have a hard day at school, have a tummy ache, are revising for an exam or fall out with a friend, etc. If they're crying or very upset or angry (and if they'll let you tap on them!) you can simply tap on them without words until the emotional intensity has dropped. Then you can start introducing words to your tapping routine.

Tapping for different age groups

Pre-conception

Yes, you read that correctly! Steps 1, 2, and 3 work really well for women who are trying to conceive. If you believe that the soul of your incoming child already exists, this will be easy. If you don't, tapping on how you feel about the fact that you haven't conceived yet will be a really good thing to do. You can also imagine or visualise your child and send them positive qualities, or do some surrogate tapping for them.

During pregnancy

There are no known contraindications for tapping on any of these points during pregnancy. However, since there is a general increased risk of miscarriage during the first three months of pregnancy some women prefer to either gently touch the points rather than tap on them, or to hover just above the points without actually touching them in their first trimester.

During pregnancy you can also make good use of Steps 1, 2 and 3. Here is an example of tapping to turn a breech baby.

> A mum in labour with a breech baby called me from the hospital asking if I could help her turn the baby to avoid a caesarean birth. I told her I didn't know if I could help, but was happy to give it a try. I'd been told by a wise and experienced midwife that babies sometimes turn to the breech position because they want their head to be close to their mother's heart, particularly if the mother is experiencing sadness or grief. I tested out this hypothesis by asking the mum if this resonated with her. It did, so we tapped for the baby, reassuring her that her mother was well and being supported through her sadness, that the sadness belonged to her mum, not to her, and that her mother loved her very much. I'm pleased to say that the baby turned during the session, as confirmed by a scan, and they were able to have a natural birth.

Many mums also find the following process very comforting when they're experiencing stress or other negative emotions and are concerned about them affecting their baby.

Put one hand on your belly and tap through the points with the other, starting at the top of your head, saying the following statements to your baby:

❋ These feelings are mine, not yours
❋ I'm so sorry you're experiencing them too
❋ They aren't your fault, and they're nothing to do with you
❋ I'm releasing them through tapping
❋ You're safe
❋ I love you very much and I can't wait to meet you

Please adapt these words to express your own feelings.

For babies

Steps 1 to 4 work well with babies. If you're tapping on a baby it can be done with the gentlest pressure, or simply by touching each point gently and taking a deep breath. You can tap with or without words. If you're tapping with words, you could tap on your baby while saying what you imagine she or he is thinking or feeling. Here's an example tapping routine:

Tapping script example for an overtired baby

Side of hand: Even though you're feeling so tired, you're a gorgeous baby and I love you so much.

Even though you just can't fall asleep, you're a wonderful baby and I love you all the way to the moon and back.

Even though you're feeling overtired and frustrated that sleep isn't coming, you're safe, and you can relax now.

Top of head: So tired.
Eyebrow: So frustrated.
Side of eye: Can't fall asleep.
Under eye: Exhausted.
Under nose: Overtired.
Chin: You just want to get to sleep.
Collarbone: I wish I could help you.
Under arm: I love you so much.

Top of head: You're warm and safe.
Eyebrow: You can relax now.
Side of eye: Allow your eyes to gently close.
Under eye: Let your body relax.
Under nose: Soften your muscles.
Chin: Easy sleep.
Collarbone: Relaxed sleep.
Under arm: Deep sleep.
Chest: [taking a deep breath] Transform.

The youngest child I've tapped with was my four-month-old nephew. We were visiting my sister-in-law and her family and she told me that her little boy hadn't been feeding well for the past 48 hours. After suggesting all the usual mum stuff, I asked if she'd like me to tap on him. She agreed, so while she held him I tapped very gently on his points without any words. After about five minutes he started rooting and wanting to latch on. My sister-in-law gave him a feed and then he fell into a peaceful sleep.

For younger children

The best time to introduce tapping to younger children is when they're calm. If they're in the middle of a tantrum or a strop they're unlikely to allow you to tap on them. My suggestion is to introduce it as part of the bedtime routine. As you tuck your child into bed you can take their hand and lightly tap on their finger points as they tell you about their day. That way they can release the day, calm their mind and fall asleep easily. If they're preverbal you can recount their day for them, including the difficult bits so that they can be acknowledged and released. If tapping seems a bit odd to them at bedtime, you could also simply touch the finger points and take a deep breath between each point. Here's a lovely story from Sarah about how tapping helped her daughter:

> My daughter struggles to settle to sleep, and last night she felt scared of the dark. I suggested she think happy thoughts and 'change the channel' in her mind. When this didn't work I asked her if she'd like to do some tapping, as it helps her to relax. I gently tapped through the points as she lay in bed. After the second round she said 'Mum! I just thought a happy thought! I imagined a cat angel!' She went to sleep peacefully after that.

When introducing EFT, imagery can often help. This is what one EFT practitioner did:

> Clare described to her daughter how difficult emotions are like fire. Using the image of a thermometer, she helped her gauge the level of the fire's heat (the intensity of her emotions). Then she described tapping as a jug of water being poured over the part of the brain that manages the emotions, which can overheat. Cooling the brain can help it to get on with its functions, such as doing maths and reading at school.

Tapping for older children

You'll probably need to give older children an age-appropriate explanation to get them on board with tapping. There are some research articles listed under Further resources on page 275. It will help if you explain that tapping can be used to help them focus, release procrastination, stress and anxiety before exams, heartbreak and jealousy about boy/friend/girlfriend problems, anxiety about their appearance, feeling antagonistic to their parents etc.

Example tapping script for older children

This is just an example: adapt it to suit your child's situation and feelings.

Side of hand:	Even though I'm worried about the exam tomorrow, I'm okay. Even though I know I haven't done enough revision, I'm open to the possibility of letting some of this anxiety go. Even though it's too late to do anything about it, I know that a calm mind will help.
Top of head:	Worried.
Eyebrow:	Anxious.
Side of eye:	Nervous.
Under eye:	Scared.
Under nose:	I haven't done enough revision.
Chin:	Annoyed with myself.
Collarbone:	Not clever enough.
Under arm:	Scared of failing.
Top of head:	Stressed.
Eyebrow:	Secretly I want to do well.
Side of eye:	But I'm scared I'm not good enough.
Under eye:	I wonder if I could feel a bit calmer than this.
Under nose:	I wonder if I could feel a bit more relaxed than this.
Chin:	I'm open to the possiblity of feeling those feelings.
Collarbone:	Calm and relaxation bring more focus and clarity.
Under arm:	Clarity and focus allow me to present my knowledge to the best of my ability.
Chest:	[taking a deep breath] Transform.

Teresa's story

Surrogate Tapping

I was driving my daughter to school and we had a conversation about her being shy and not showing her skills and abilities in class. I told her I had the impression she was hiding and playing down her talent. She told me she didn't like showing off and that she did not want to. By the time I dropped her off at school the connection between us had dropped and I was feeling miserable.

So I started tapping and did surrogate tapping for about ten minutes. It led to a great insight and a sense of lightness where I was able to let go of my ego.

Then I tapped on my need for her to be popular and successful to cover my own lack of it (I got here before I could really think about my hidden agenda, and this was an unexpected revelation!)

I tapped saying 'I set you free to be the way you want to be. I take responsibility for my needs.'

At this point I started feeling lighter as I came to accept that my daughter may not want to be that popular in school, and that's her choice. I found peace and it feels like I'm a better parent (than I was before tapping!)

When I went to pick my daughter up in the afternoon she said that in the morning she'd participated in a public talk at the town hall, where she'd gone with the school. The topic was how to improve the town. She'd made her intervention in front of more than 50 people, and when she finished she'd got applause and a handshake from some government officers who were very impressed by her speech!

It sounded incredible to me, as we hadn't known this trip to the town hall was scheduled and it had all just happened out of the blue. I believe that by tapping on my needs and taking responsibility for my own success, I freed space around my daughter so that she could bloom with her own light. Absolutely amazing!

As an EFT practitioner this experience gave me the confidence to treat children's issues by treating the parent first.

Next steps

Throughout this book you've been tapping using my scripts or videos. But I don't want you to depend on me: I want you to be able to tap on anything, anytime, anywhere! I also want you to get deep, permanent results, not just daily boosts of de-stressing or pockets of relaxation.

Using EFT without a script

I encourage you to experiment with your wording as you tap. When you use words that match what you're feeling and what you want to feel you'll get the best results. The more specific you can be in what you're saying, the more effective the tapping will be. Tapping using scripts and videos is just the tip of the iceberg in terms of what's possible with EFT.

Here are some ways you can nurture yourself more deeply, with long-lasting results:

❋ Download our free EFT manual from Frazzledtofabulous.com/Bonus. You can read it in your own time and do the exercises to release emotions from past memories and experiences, learn how to use EFT for cravings and addictions, and lots more

❋ Join my online club for mums at Frazzledtofabulous.com/Bonus and receive mum-related tapping videos in your inbox

❋ Attend a live workshop: my husband and I run these online, in the UK and occasionally in other places including the US,

Singapore and Dubai. See the Appendix on page 281 for workshops in your area. Participants get direct experience of the deeper processes for releasing trauma, core issues, the emotional aspects of physical conditions, Energy EFT, and goal-setting

❀ Book a one-to-one session. See the Appendix on page 281 for a link to the list of registered EFT International Accredited EFT Practitioners

Digging deeper

You probably bought this book because you hadn't been addressing your needs. Once you've established a daily tapping habit you'll be able to start addressing other areas of your life to create optimum wellbeing without the pressure of overwhelm or stress. Returning to the plant analogy, a plant needs optimal light and temperature, the right kind of soil, and repotting every so often. What do *you* need for an optimal life?

When you work on clearing the underlying reasons and roots of your stress, anxiety and overwhelm you'll be removing the repeating patterns that cause them in the first place. You may think that the reason for your stress is lack of support from your partner and children, having to look after elderly parents, or trying to juggle a full-time job with childcare, etc. Although these may seem to be causing your stress, different people respond to identical situations in different ways. One mum might thrive in a full-time job and feel fulfilled in the time she spends with her family at home; another might resent having to work full-time, and yet another might feel overwhelmed because everything falls on her shoulders. It's the story you tell yourself about your situation rather than the situation itself that's the problem. EFT will help you change your story about your situation, and then if you still don't like the situation you'll have released the negative emotions about it, giving you more clarity about how to change it.

Many of the stories mums create about their situations are connected to or caused by things that did or didn't happen when they were young. If your mum told you that having children is a bad idea and she was always stressed and overwhelmed, that didn't paint a positive picture of motherhood. You might unconsciously decide to make it right for your children by trying to be the mum you didn't have. That decision would put constant pressure on you and your parenting without you even being aware of it.

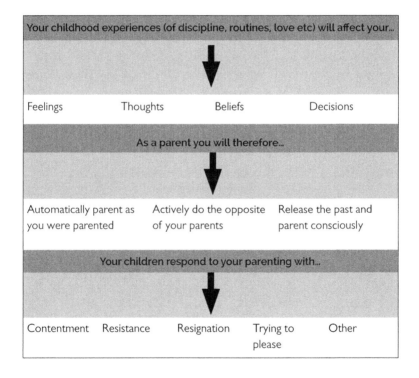

The diagram above shows how your childhood experiences influenced your thoughts, feelings, beliefs and decisions. Take a child who was heavily disciplined, for example. He may have felt fearful and believed 'I'm bad' or 'I'm unlovable because I make my parents angry,' which could lead him to decide to be a good, helpful and kind boy and not rock the boat, doing everything to keep the peace at home. This is just one outcome of strong parental discipline. Another child might become defiant and push even harder against her parents, which would give rise to a completely different set of beliefs.

The beliefs and decisions that you formed as a child consciously or subconsciously affect the way you parent. The most common scenarios are parenting exactly as your parents did, especially if it was a positive experience, or deciding that you will do the opposite. A person who was heavily disciplined as a child, and as a result always feels the need to keep the peace, may decide to take the opposite approach and be completely relaxed and laid-back about disciplining her children. While she continues to hold on to negative emotions such as fear or resentment and limiting beliefs such as 'I'm bad' or 'I'm unlovable', due to the way she was brought up, she will parent from a place of pain and suffering and her children will pick up on this at some level. She may even hear her parent's words coming out of her own mouth – the very words that she swore she would never repeat. So although she consciously parents her children in exactly the opposite way to how her parents brought her up, unconsciously she will perpetuate discipline challenges until a child further down the family line is able to release this pattern. If you think about your own family, you may notice commonly-expressed comments such as 'In our family we always do this/act like this…' or 'This situation has always been a challenge in our family,' etc.

Working with an EFT practitioner it's possible to address the underlying factors that contribute to your parenting challenges. The practitioner can help you to gently and sensitively explore your childhood experiences and release negative emotions and limiting beliefs about yourself and your parenting, allowing you to create new ways of parenting that are neither too strict nor too laid-back.

Children interpret how they are parented in their own way. It may be understood as the parents intend or taken in a totally different and unexpected way. As parents we can have the best intentions in the world, but we have no control over how our children will interpret them. What we can do, however, is tap on how we feel when our children misinterpret our well-intended actions, for instance if we feel guilty about how we parented them or how they interpreted our positive intentions in a negative way.

For example, my husband and I have always supported our daughter with her challenges by doing some tapping with her. However, she recently said to us 'Let me have my problems – you make me feel like it's not okay to have problems!' We can laugh about it, but it's interesting to see how our good intentions to help her through her difficulties were misinterpreted. She felt pressurised, and that we weren't accepting her as she was and were trying to improve her. She's still happy to tap, but only on her terms – which is exactly as it should be.

What else can EFT be used for?

You've discovered that EFT is great for releasing stress and other negative emotions, as well as for increasing your sense of joy. By tapping for five minutes a day every day you've probably noticed areas of your life outside parenting changing. A series of sessions with an experienced EFT practitioner can speed up the changes you notice and dramatically reduce the likelihood of your problems returning. Some other areas that EFT can be used for include:

❊ negative emotions, eg anger, fear, anxiety
❊ limiting beliefs such as 'I'm not good enough,' 'life's a struggle'
❊ goals, eg trying to conceive, lose weight, improve at a sport

❀ emotional causes of physical pain, eg anger that the van drove into me, leaving me with chronic pain

❀ addictions, eg to sugar, coffee, screen time, smoking

❀ post-traumatic stress following experience of war, traumatic birth, etc

❀ upsetting memories, eg accident, divorce, bereavement

❀ during labour, eg for pain, fear, exhaustion

The list is endless!

What are you going to do to keep EFT going in your own and your children's lives?

Now that you've come to the end of the book, the last thing I want for you is that you go back to the way you were. What steps can you put in place to keep this fabulous momentum going?

Here are some suggestions:

❀ Don't beat yourself up if you forget to tap

❀ Set a specific amount of time for tapping at the same hour each day

❀ Set yourself up for success. Don't try to do more than you can comfortably manage each day, even if that's just one minute

❀ Get an accountability buddy who you can message each day when you've done your daily tapping and for mutual support when you forget to tap or are having a hard time

❀ Tap with a friend, your partner or your child

❀ If you don't know how to express what you want to tap on, choose a video from the many available on YouTube

❀ If you don't know what to tap on today, ask yourself what negative emotion you're experiencing right now and tap on that. If you're feeling fabulous, ask yourself what you would need to feel even more fabulous!

Troubleshooting

If you're using EFT for the first time you may find it takes a while to adjust to it and for it to work. Let me assure you that many of the mums taking my challenge who had never used these techniques before now use them every time they feel stressed. It has become a daily habit to support their wellbeing and a parenting tool that they share with their children.

If you're reading this, I'm guessing that you didn't get the results you were expecting from using one or more of the tapping scripts. Below are some tips to help you.

Over 80 per cent of my clients notice improvement with EFT quickly and easily. Another 10 per cent improve with perseverance, and the remaining 10 per cent could benefit from the support of an EFT practitioner.

With a few exceptions, most of the tapping scripts in this book address negative aspects of your life. When tapping on something negative you're aiming to reduce the intensity of your emotion, ideally to 0 on a scale of 0 to 10. When tapping on your level of wellbeing by focusing on something positive such as your Blissful Day, you're aiming to increase the intensity of your feelings towards 10 on the scale.

If the intensity of your emotion hasn't changed or you're feeling worse after tapping whether you're focusing on a positive or negative issue, this chapter will offer you some hints and tips for improving your results.

For mums who doubt the effect of EFT

Okay, I know it's weird! You might be thinking something like 'How can tapping on parts of your face while saying some words make any difference to my problems?' Or 'You don't know me and my particular problem of juggling a sick child, a job I hate, multiple school runs, a husband who's never home and a mother-in-law who keeps comparing my parenting with the way she thinks it should be done!'

You're right; I don't know you, but I do know that this system has worked for hundreds of mums in all sorts of challenging situations.

EFT works best when your mind is on board with it, and it's possible that right now yours isn't. It may have all sorts of objections. The thoughts created in your mind may be a constant chatter of criticism that:

* prevents you accessing your creativity
* obscures solutions to moving forward with clarity and joy
* requires a lot of self-control to shut it down
* makes you easily distracted

When I find my scattered and negative thoughts interfering with my tapping, as occasionally happens, I ask my mind to lie on a hammock on a beach, relax and read a book. I actually have a memory of doing this on a beautiful white sandy beach in the Maldives, so thinking about it, even now as I write, makes me take a deep, relaxing breath.

The next step is to tap on any objections your mind might be throwing up, such as 'Tapping is stupid,' 'It's a waste of time,' 'I'm too busy for this,' or whatever thoughts are arising. Here's a tapping script to help you get started. Use your own words to describe exactly what you're feeling for the best results.

Tapping script for people who don't believe in EFT

Side of hand: Even though EFT is weird and I don't believe it can work, I accept myself and my beliefs.

Even though I feel silly and self-conscious tapping and saying these words, I accept myself and my thoughts about this and I'm open to the possibility of suspending my disbelief and having a go!

Even though my mind is interfering with my goal of feeling calmer, I choose to give it a relaxing break reading its favourite book in a hammock on a beach.

Top of head: EFT is rubbish!

Eyebrow: It doesn't work.

Side of eye: I feel silly.

Under eye: I feel self-conscious.

Under nose: It's weird!

Chin: How can it possibly work?

Collarbone: I want to feel different.

Under arm: But I don't see how tapping on a few points on my body can make a difference!

Top of head: But for some reason I'm tapping anyway.

Eyebrow: My negative thoughts are getting in the way.

Side of eye: My scepticism is getting in the way.

Under eye: But I'm struggling with my life at the moment.

Under nose: And nothing else has made any difference.

Chin: So I'm open to the possibility of giving this a chance.

Collarbone: I've got nothing to lose.

Under arm:	I've got everything to gain.
Top of head:	This is the first step.
Eyebrow:	I'm open to new possibilities for starting over.
Side of eye:	I'm open to feeling some calm and peace.
Under eye:	I'm open to feeling some ease and relaxation.
Under nose:	I'm open to being able to prioritise and be productive.
Chin:	I'm open to having a better relationship with my children.
Collarbone:	I'm open to being unexpectedly surprised.
Under arm:	I'm ready to change for good.
Chest:	[taking a deep breath] Transform.

Difficulty rating your issue with a number

Some people find it hard to rate their problem on a numerical scale. Others worry they may get the number wrong. However, this rating is subjective, and you can't get it wrong. If you can tell what number represents the intensity of your feeling, simply guess. Guessing works just as well in my experience. Having said that, some people prefer to rate their intensity in other ways, which are also subjective and also work well. These alternatives are particularly useful with children, especially if they haven't yet learnt to count.

Using colours

You may prefer to choose a colour to represent how you feel before and after tapping. If the colour changes, this shows that EFT has evolved the problem. If you continue tapping, keep noticing the colour changes until you feel Calm, Light And Peaceful (CLAP!). In my experience with clients, the colour usually evolves to white.

Using the space between your hands

Alternatively, you can hold your hands apart in front of you to express the size of the problem. The further apart, the bigger the problem. As the problem reduces in intensity the distance between your hands shrinks.

I'm too stressed to tap!

If you're feeling so stressed, overwhelmed or exhausted that you can't think straight or read the daily challenge, don't worry – just follow this SOS process.

The SOS process

This is a very simple exercise from a variation of EFT called Energy EFT, and only takes a few seconds. I introduced it on Day 2 of the Challenge, but here's a reminder. Put your hands, one on top of the other, in the centre of your chest and take at least three (ideally more) long, deep breaths until you feel calmer. If you find breathing deeply uncomfortable, simply breathe normally until you feel calmer. You could try putting your hands in the centre of your chest and saying to yourself:

✽ 'De-stress' (taking a deep breath)
✽ 'Accepting my stress' (taking a deep breath)
✽ 'Accepting myself in this situation' (taking a deep breath)
✽ 'All is well in my world' (taking a deep breath)

Only say what feels comfortable and right for you, replacing my words with ones that feel more relevant if necessary.

If you feel able to return to the daily challenge, start now. If it's too much for the moment, don't worry. You're a work in progress, and that's okay. Try creating some space for yourself, maybe even relaxing in the bath, bringing the book with you, and see if you can try the tapping again.

I've fallen behind!

That's okay. It happens to all of us with the best will in the world – but that's not a reason to give up! Simply go back to where you've got to and continue. If you often find yourself falling behind, the following story may help. It's an adaptation of the story 'Autobiography in Five Chapters' by Portia Nelson, in Sogyal Rinpoche's *Tibetan Book of Living and Dying*.

The Mum Who Fell Down a Hole

Chapter 1

One day a mum walks down a street, juggling so many balls that she doesn't see the deep hole in the pavement and falls into it. She feels frustrated, lost and hopeless. It's not her fault. It takes her forever to find a way out.

Chapter 2

The next day she walks down the same street. There's still a deep hole in the pavement. She pretends she doesn't see it coming. She falls in again. She can't believe she's in the same place: she was hoping things would turn out differently this time. She feels frustrated

at her children, her partner and her life. She wants to give her children a happy childhood and spend quality time at home, at work, with her partner and even with herself, but somehow it never turns out that way. It takes her takes a long time to get out.

Chapter 3

The next day she walks down the same street. There's still a deep hole in the pavement. She sees it there: and falls in anyway! It's a habit. It's the story of her life. She tries all sorts of different things such as distracting herself with

chocolate and wine, trying yoga, getting a massage, but still life continues in an annoying and uncomfortable repetitive pattern with never enough time, energy or patience for her children, her work, her home, her partner or herself.

She falls in with her eyes wide open. She knows where she is. She knows it's her fault. Irritated with herself, she remembers the way out and takes it.

Chapter 4

The next day she walks down the same street. There's the deep hole in the pavement. She sees it. Maybe she does some tapping! She walks around it.

Chapter 5

She walks down another
street.

Can you relate to this story? I, and many mums I know, can. As
humans we tend to repeat the same patterns over and over until we
get the message and change our behaviour. As I mentioned earlier,
Einstein said that the definition of insanity is doing the same thing
over and over again and expecting a different result.

When we walk down the same street again and again without
looking where we're going because our minds are cluttered with
our to-do lists, worrying about what we can rustle up for dinner and
trying to remember if we locked the front door this morning, it's
understandable that we won't see the hole in the pavement.

The good news is that EFT can help you to

❀ become aware of the hole (the negative patterns in your life)
❀ feel compassion for yourself when you fall into the hole –
because you will!
❀ clear your mind so that you can find strategies for getting out of
the hole
❀ get out of the hole faster than you would have been able to
otherwise
❀ release the limiting beliefs and behaviours that are causing you to
fall down the hole in the first place
❀ avoid the hole – and eventually walk down another street

Sarah, a regular tapping mum, shared with the Facebook group:

> 'Goodness, I nearly fell into the hole of not tapping today – I
> was too busy!!! then I thought 'NO, I'm too busy NOT to tap!'
> After the tapping I'm now so ramped up to crack on I can hardly
> sit still long enough to type this, so excuse my brevity! Buzzing
> buzzing buzzing I love tapping.'

I feel worse!

If you're feeling worse than when you started, don't worry! It's
probably because feelings that you've pushed away and repressed are
coming to the surface. This is a good sign, because once they come
into your conscious awareness you can acknowledge and release
them using EFT. Repeat the tapping script as many times as necessary
until you feel the intensity of the emotion dropping. If it still doesn't
go down, use the SOS process described on page 48. If you're still
struggling, do join the Facebook group at Frazzledtofabulous.com/
Bonus to access some support.

Feeling no different?

If nothing at all has changed after tapping, read on.

After tapping people often feel

* tired
* energised
* calm or peaceful
* emotional – generally in a good way!
* tingling
* heavy
* lighter
* and more…

Yawning, sighing and (yes, I know it's a bit weird) burping are all signs that your energy is moving and EFT is working.

Sometimes mums report not feeling anything at all after tapping, but the next day they wake up happier and more positive.

Self-sabotage

If your rating on the scale hasn't changed, it's most likely due to self-sabotage. Here are a few simple tips that often help to release this pattern and neutralise self-sabotaging behaviour at least for a few minutes, allowing you to use EFT to move beyond the resistance.

Tip 1: The SOS process as described on Day 2

Put your hands in the centre of your chest and take a few deep breaths. If you came to this section because you were struggling with a tapping script, try it again now or choose another topic that you feel more aligned with to tap on.

Tip 2: Be specific

EFT works most effectively when the words you say closely match what you're feeling. The words of the tapping scripts in this book represent the types of issue my clients tell me about and are fairly general. Not all of my statements will be relevant to you. You'll have your own particular version of stress, overwhelm, or whatever you're here to change, so once you're used to the EFT process I encourage you to adapt my words if necessary to reflect your own reality.

For example, if you're tapping on your anxiety saying 'Even though I have this anxiety, I deeply and completely accept myself' you may get a result, but you're likely to get a better result if you're more specific:

1. Focus on a specific event in your life when the emotion, in this case anxiety, was strong. It's even better if you can remember the first time you ever felt this way: 'Even though I feel anxious when I think about the time I didn't know if he was coming home or not...'

2. Focus on where you feel the feeling in your body and its colour, texture, size and any other detail you can imagine or see: 'Even though I have this blue, achy anxiety on the left side of my chest...'

3. Combine both of the above, in this example by focusing on the colour, texture, size etc of the anxiety and where you feel it in your body when you think about the time you didn't know if he was coming home: 'Even though I have this blue, achy anxiety on the left side of my chest when I think about the time I didn't know if he was coming home or not...'

Tip 3: Add emphasis

Say the setup phrase with emphasis – loudly and with meaning! Stand up and shout it: anything to add strength to how you're expressing your feeling.

Tip 4: The Sore Spot

Instead of tapping on the side of the hand at the start of the script, rub the Sore Spot. Locate it about 3 inches (8 centimetres) below and about 3 inches to the left or right of the dip in your throat. As the name suggests, feel for a spot that is sensitive and feels sore when you press it. The Sore Spot is lower down and further from the midline of the body than the Collarbone Point. Continue tapping through the remaining points as usual.

Tip 5: Find and address limiting beliefs

Ask yourself the following questions and use the answers to build a tapping statement:

❋ If I had a reason for wanting to keep this problem, what would it be?

❋ If I had a reason for not wanting to let this problem go, what would it be?

For example, many mums I know are caught in the vicious cycle of having too much to do in too little time. Here are some of their beliefs about themselves and their situations that were preventing them from being able to find a solution:

❋ It's just the way it is, and it's the way it was when I was growing up

❋ Mothers can't have it all

❋ I have to do it all myself

❋ Everyone else has things under control, so what's wrong with me?

❋ If I can't do it all it means I'm weak, so I *have* to do it all!

These are limiting beliefs, and they can cause us to stop looking for solutions or to push ourselves harder to keep going, all the while getting more and more exhausted and impatient with our children. Even if solutions present themselves we may be unable to see them.

For example, your mum, a kind neighbour or a friend offers to mind your child for a few hours while you take a nap or get some stuff done, but you refuse because you're not used to receiving help, and you keep plodding on. Or you refuse because you feel it's a sign of weakness – your mum did it all herself, so you should be able to as well.

You can use the limiting beliefs you uncover in your tapping round. For example, as you tap on the side of your hand or rub the sore spot, say:

Even though my mum did it all herself and I should be able to too, I choose to accept myself and this situation.

Repeat this three times. Then tap through the points in the usual way, alternating between 'My mum did it all herself' and 'I should be able to too'.

Tip 6: Tap on the same issue twice or more, as time permits.

One way of working with stubborn issues is to use persistence. EFT can work both impressively fast or with persistent tapping over time. The key is to be patient and gentle with yourself. If time allows, repeat the daily tapping scripts twice or more in a row or set aside five minutes both in the morning and in the evening; or you could spend a couple of minutes tapping every time you go to the loo.

Why do I have to make negative statements?

The reason EFT uses negative statements is to help you acknowledge what you're already feeling. In the moment when uncomfortable feelings arise, it is sometimes easier to bury them and present a strong or positive front. When you're in a stressful situation that demands action, there isn't space for what you're feeling. When an animal is hunted and gets away, it shakes for a period of time to release the fear and stress. We humans don't do that: we just carry on, pushing the stress down and allowing it to accumulate.

However, if there's a continual pattern of pushing down hard-to-accept feelings they remain stored in the body and can erupt as bouts of anger, sadness, resentment, or depression, and even as physical symptoms. It's like pushing them under the carpet: although you can't see them they're still under there, making bumps or even mountains. When asked her opinion about making negative statements when using EFT, Louise Hay, the queen of affirmations, responded: 'If you want to clean your kitchen, you need to look at the dirt.' This doesn't mean you need to roll around in the dirt – you just need to acknowledge it. Looking at the dirt involves saying it how it is, for instance 'I haven't got any time' or 'I'm feeling scared/upset about this situation.' It can feel uncomfortable, but saying these statements while tapping reduces the intensity of the negative emotions until they're released completely.

If you've been working hard over the years to change negative thought patterns and statements into positive ones, you might try tapping on these statements:

> Even though I've worked so hard over the years to change my negative thought patterns into positive ones, and it's making a difference but I'm still experiencing some negative thoughts, I deeply and completely accept myself.

> Even though I'd love to feel more positive, and I'm making progress but part of me is still repeating those old hard-to-change negative thoughts, I deeply and completely accept myself and my hard-to-change thoughts.

> Even though I still have some of those old negative thought patterns left, I'm open to acknowledging and celebrating how far I've come with changing my thoughts, and the positive impact it's having on my life.

If you're still struggling...

If you're still struggling, share your experience with the Facebook group at Frazzledtofabulous.com/Bonus, and I or one of the other participants will try to help. The chances are that others are experiencing the same thing but are too shy to ask the group for help.

Have a look at Frazzledtofabulous.com/Bonus for sources of further support. If you want to find a local practitioner, the Further resources section of this book on page 275 will help.

Want to know even more about EFT?

Download our free manual or attend an EFT workshop: there are details of how to access these at Frazzledtofabulous.com/Bonus.

Further resources

For free and purchasable resources, including those listed below, go to Frazzledtofabulous.com/Bonus.

Free resources

Accountability and support group:

- ❋ Facebook support group
- ❋ Day 3 and Day 30 questionnaires
- ❋ Free EFT manual

Videos including one on how to do EFT

Printables

- ❋ Image illustrating the tapping points
- ❋ Reminder to tap

Purchasable resources

- ❋ Frazzled to Fabulous Mums' Membership Club
- ❋ Frazzled to Fabulous in 5 Minutes a Day Workbook
- ❋ Frazzled to Fabulous Fast Track to Freedom personal and group programmes

EFT training

- ❋ The EFT Training Centre, run by Peter Donn and myself, offers training online, in the UK and occasionally in the US, Singapore and Dubai. We are Master Trainers for EFT International. See eft-courses.org.uk

EFT organisations

* EFT International: eftinternational.org
* Guild of Energists (GOE): goe.ac
* EFT Universe: eftuniverse.com
* Association for Comprehensive Energy Psychology (ACEP): energypsych.org
* Gary Craig Official EFT™ training centre: emofree.com

EFT science and research

* Craig Weiner, Science of Tapping: scienceoftapping.com
* Peta Stapleton, author of *The Science Behind Tapping*: petastapleton.com/the-science-behind-tapping
* Research section of the EFT International website: eftinternational.org

Other great EFT resources

* The Tapping Solution. Unmissable annual tapping summit plus lots of other resources: thetappingsolution.com
* Brad Yates, the world's most prolific creator of tapping videos: bradyates.net

About Tamara

I help stressed, overwhelmed and exhausted mums to create new habits that allow them to be more present with their children and more productive with their time, and to experience greater peace and wellbeing. I use a host of different tools including EFT (Emotional Freedom Techniques), also known as tapping, and family constellations, as well as drawing on my own experience as a mum, wife, daughter and mumpreneur.

I run the EFT Training Centre with my husband, Peter Donn, and am the founder of the Birth Art Café,™ a holistic preparation for motherhood.

My Frazzled to Fabulous Turning Point

About ten years ago as I was driving along a busy dual carriageway my accelerator suddenly stopped working. I had no choice but to pull over as the car came to a standstill and phone for help. The RAC said there would be a two-hour wait. With no hard shoulder, the noise and fumes from the cars whizzing by very close to me were overpowering and terrifying. The RAC suggested that I call the police if I couldn't wait, so I did. Weirdly enough, the policewoman who came was able to start my car straight away!

When I got home and told Peter what had happened, he repeated my words: 'The faster I was trying to go, the slower I was going!' I realised with a shock that this was a metaphor for how I was living my life. It was a wakeup call, and I realised that something had to change. I was constantly on the go. At night, although I lay in bed, I spent my nights overthinking about my never-ending to-do list. I was fuelled by adrenalin, never stopping until my body forced me to, usually with a migraine. My car experience was a wakeup call. I felt as if a mirror had been held up to the way I was living my life, and suddenly I could clearly see that it was not conducive to a happy, easy and peaceful existence.

But how could I do things differently? I had to work, create an income, take care of my daughter and my home. Like most working mums I was juggling it all and getting nothing done well. But worst of all, I was spending most of my time not being present in the task I was doing in the moment, particularly when I was with my daughter.

It's been a long journey and it's still a work in progress, but the good news is that the structures I've put in place are working for me more of the time, the times of feeling stressed are fewer and shorter, and I often remember to use the tools and strategies that I've put in place to support myself.

The tools I use to support myself as a working mum

Luckily I work for myself, so I can choose how I use my time. I used to do most of my work while my daughter was at school so that I could be with her when she got home. As she got older and had more homework, we sometimes sat working together at the table. During the holidays I dedicated some of my time to working and the rest to making myself available to her, or doing activities as a family. Now she's an adult, I celebrate the times she wants to spend with us and try to drop everything else when they arise. I start my day with a combination of EFT, meditation, my gratitude journal, exercise, and going to the allotment – although not all on the same day! To motivate myself during the day I select one or more of the following: tap, dance, walk, say some affirmations, or a combination of all of these, depending on my mood. On workshop days I'm still finding my way to balancing my still time with all the preparations and facilitation that are required.

The primary key to creating a great start to my day is EFT. Even when I'm exhausted, overwhelmed or feeling ill, I spend at least five minutes tapping when the alarm goes off and it always improves my mood, even if only temporarily. When I do this, my days flow better and are more fun, and I get more done. On days when I forget, I notice the difference.

The mums I work with are also delighted by how life-changing this simple practice of tapping for five minutes first thing in the morning can be.

The beginning of my EFT parenting journey

As we sat together on by the edge of the swimming pool my daughter, then aged six, was shivering and scared of her imminent swimming lesson. I was feeling slightly helpless and was struggling to find yet another useful suggestion for her. I'd exhausted statements such as 'I can see you're scared. It's going to be okay – you know the teacher, she'll go at your pace'; 'You'll feel better when you're in the water'; 'It's only half an hour'; 'You'll be able to swim when we go on holiday;' and the even less helpful 'I've paid for it, so you have to do it!'

Then I remembered EFT – that weird thing my husband did! I took her hand and gently started tapping on her. Within a few minutes she heaved a deep sigh and said 'I'm ready now, Mummy!'

What would I do without this powerful tool? That was several years ago and I've never looked back. I loved the technique so much that I trained in EFT and now support other mothers and pregnant women with issues relating to parenting, helping them to transform their lives and succeed on their journeys.

It's really important that I walk my talk, because if I'm supporting other mums creating a harmonious life for themselves, I need to use my tools myself and know that they work.

I tell my clients that life is made up of periods of activity and periods of stillness. The active times are like breaths in, and the still times are like breaths out. If you keep doing activity after activity it's like breathing in after you've already breathed in. If you keep going without stopping (or breathing out) your body can force you to breathe out, which can manifest as a cold, a headache, period pains, or worse.

Understandably, sometimes mums with younger children find it difficult to think of their own needs when their children still need so much from them. I know I found it hard myself. But the stronger and the more centred and grounded you are, the more you can give your children. On aeroplanes parents are always told to put on their own oxygen mask before helping their children. This can be unsettling, because as parents we put our children first; however, when we take care of our own needs we have more presence, patience and energy for our children. In times gone by we lived in communities rather than as nuclear families, and there was always another member of the family or community to mind the children. Nowadays it's often one just parent shouldering the responsibility for the children or organising the childcare as well as working, making it harder for parents to take the time to meet their own needs. Doing five minutes of tapping a day is the ideal solution to lifting your energy when time is short, and the cumulative effect can create change in all areas of life.

Appendix

Tapping scripts

Your top challenge	61
I can't change!	67
Time? What time?!	73
Creating your Blissful Day: Part 1	85
Creating your Blissful Day: Part 2	90
Are you insane?	96
Can you see the wood for the trees?	102
What do elephants believe?	109
Creating your Blissful Day revisited	115
Getting it right	127
Are you being pulled in too many directions?	133
What do you deserve?	140
What are you putting off?	147
How many thoughts are bouncing around your mind right now?	153
Creating your Blissful Day revisited	159
Anxiety	171
Mothers' guilt	178
Are your baby or to-do list keeping you up at night?	186
Waking up having to hit the ground running	192
Are you present with your children?	198
Creating your Blissful Day revisited	204
I am enough	214
Celebration	223

Accepting feelings about an issue with your child   236
Sending your child positive qualities   239
Surrogate tapping for a child   242
Overtired baby   248
Older child's exam fears   251
I don't believe in EFT!   261